Street by Street

ST ALBANS

HARPENDEN, REDBOURN

Chiswell Green, Colney Heath, How Wood, London Colney, Park Street, Sandridge, Wheathampstead

2nd edition September 2007
© Automobile Association Developments Limited 2007

Original edition printed August 2002

Enabled by OS Ordnance Survey

This product includes map data licensed from Ordnance Survey® with the permission of the Controller of Her Majesty's Stationery Office. © Crown copyright 2007. All rights reserved. Licence number 100021153.

The copyright in all PAF is owned by Royal Mail Group plc.

All rights reserved. No part of this publication may be reproduced, stored in a retrieval system, or transmitted in any form or by any means – electronic, mechanical, photocopying, recording or otherwise – unless the permission of the publisher has been given beforehand.

Published by AA Publishing (a trading name of Automobile Association Developments Limited, whose registered office is Fanum House, Basing View, Basingstoke, Hampshire RG21 4EA. Registered number 1878835).

Produced by the Mapping Services Department of The Automobile Association. (A03129)

A CIP Catalogue record for this book is available from the British Library.

Printed by Oriental Press in Dubai

The contents of this atlas are believed to be correct at the time of the latest revision. However, the publishers cannot be held responsible or liable for any loss or damage occasioned to any person acting or refraining from action as a result of any use or reliance on any material in this atlas, nor for any errors, omissions or changes in such material. This does not affect your statutory rights. The publishers would welcome information to correct any errors or omissions and to keep this atlas up to date. Please write to Publishing, The Automobile Association, Fanum House (FH12), Basing View, Basingstoke, Hampshire, RG21 4EA. E-mail: *streetbystreet@theaa.com*

Ref: ML187z

Key to map symbols	ii
Key to map pages	1
Enlarged map pages	2-3
Main map pages	4-33
Index – towns & villages	34
Index – streets	35-39
Index – featured places	39-40
Acknowledgements	40

ii Map Symbols

Junction 9	Motorway & junction	
Services	Motorway service area	
	Primary road single/dual	
Services	Primary road service area	
	A road single/dual carriageway	
	B road single/dual carriageway	
	Other road single/dual carriageway	
	Minor/private road, access may be restricted	
← ←	One-way street	
	Pedestrian area	
	Track or footpath	
	Road under construction	
	Road tunnel	
P	Parking	
P+	Park & Ride	
	Bus/coach station	
	Railway & main railway station	
	Railway & minor railway station	
	Light railway & station	
	Preserved private railway	
LC	Level crossing	
	Tramway	
	Ferry route	
	Airport runway	
	County, administrative boundary	
	Mounds	
	City wall	

17	Page continuation 1:15,000	
2	Page continuation to enlarged scale 1:10,000	
	River/canal, lake, pier	
	Aqueduct, lock, weir	
465 Winter Hill	Peak (with height in metres)	
	Beach	
	Woodland	
	Park	
	Cemetery	
	Built-up area	
	Industrial/business building	
	Leisure building	
	Retail building	
	Other building	
Madeira Hotel	Hotel AA inspected	
A&E	Hospital with 24-hour A&E department	
PO	Post Office	
	Public library	
i	Tourist Information Centre	
i	Seasonal Tourist Information Centre	
	Petrol station, 24 hour Major suppliers only	
†	Church/chapel	
	Public toilets	
	Toilet with disabled facilities	
PH	Public house AA recommended	
	Restaurant AA inspected	
	Theatre or performing arts centre	

	Cinema	
	Golf course	
	Camping AA inspected	
	Caravan site AA inspected	
	Camping & caravan site AA inspected	
	Theme park	
	Abbey, cathedral or priory	
	Castle	
	Historic house or building	
Wakehurst Place NT	National Trust property	
M	Museum or art gallery	
	Roman antiquity	
	Ancient site, battlefield or monument	
	Industrial interest	
	Garden	
	Garden Centre Garden Centre Association Member	
	Garden Centre Wyevale Garden Centre	
	Arboretum	
	Farm or animal centre	
	Zoological or wildlife collection	
	Bird collection	
	Nature reserve	
V	Visitor or heritage centre	
	Country park	
	Cave	
	Windmill	
	Distillery, brewery or vineyard	

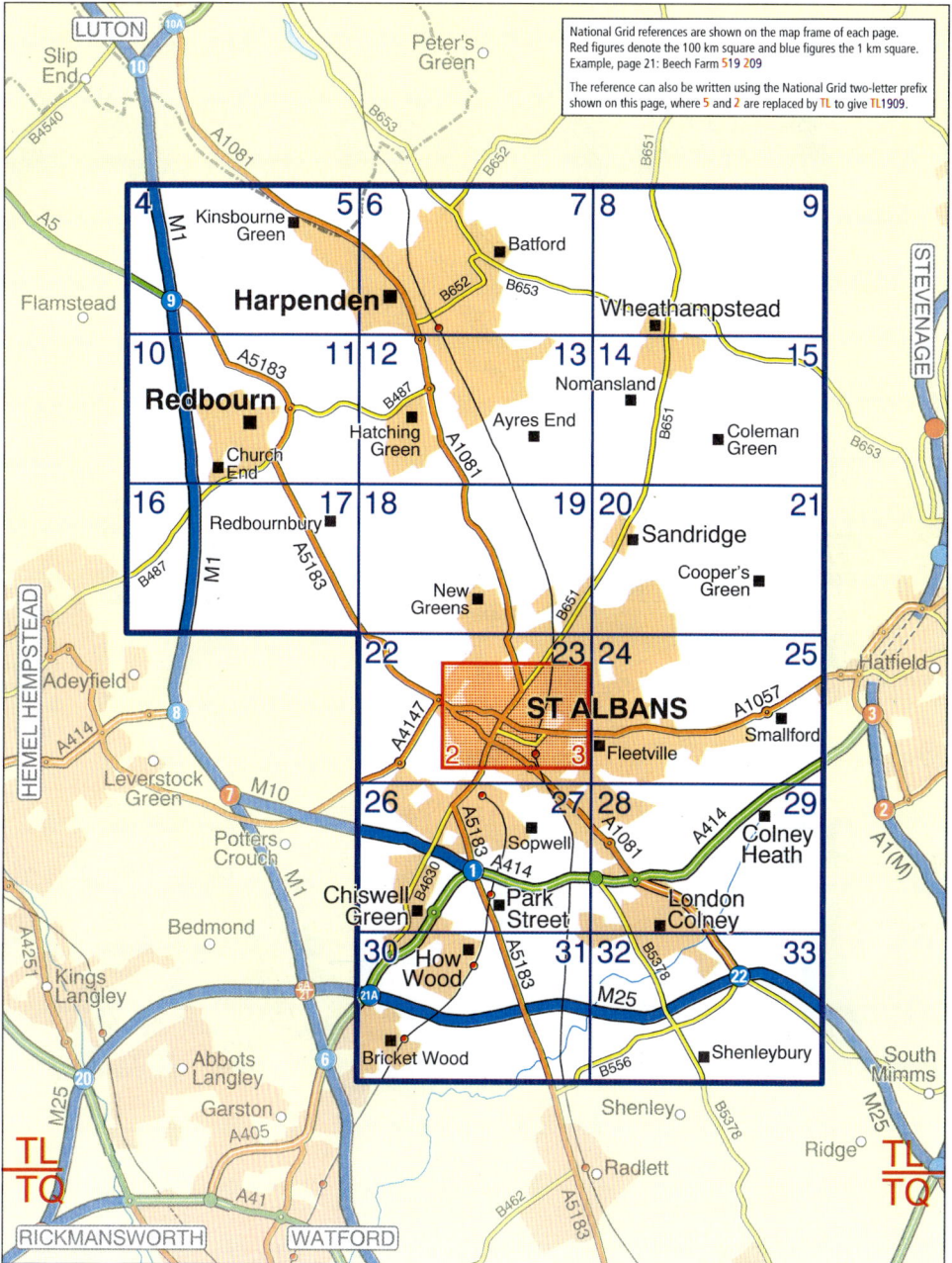

National Grid references are shown on the map frame of each page.
Red figures denote the 100 km square and blue figures the 1 km square.
Example, page 21: Beech Farm 519 209

The reference can also be written using the National Grid two-letter prefix
shown on this page, where 5 and 2 are replaced by TL to give TL1909.

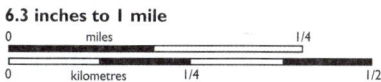

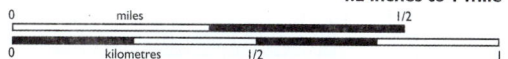

A B 22 C D E

514

I

Townsend

ST A

Batchwood Drive
Links View
Grove
White Hedge Drive
Everlasting Lane
Ladies
Everlasting Lane
Oysterfields
Dormie Close
Temple View
Oysterfields

2
3

Waverley Road
Langley
High Gv View
Batchwood Av
Eleanor
Margaret Av
Alban Avenue
Lavender Crs
Chene Drive
Pegasus Pl
PO
Augusta St
Townsend Drive
Ltr Acre
Heydons Close
Gorse Corner
May Cl
Townsend Drive
Edmund Beaufort Dr
Heat

St Albans City Hospital
Surgery
Works
Newmarket Ct
Goldsmith Way
Calmont Way
Kimberley Rd
Ladysmith Rd
Normandy
Waverley Road
Palfrey Close
Carlisle
Heath Av
St Bernard's Rd
Towns
Surgery
Hall

HARPENDEN ROAD
Heathland

JMI School
St Albans Music Sch
Grimthorpe Close
Beckett's Rd
Langley
Crescent
Como Rd

AL3

Downedge
VERULAN
22
Camlet Way
Fryth Mead
Branch Rd
Kingsbury Avenue
The Lawns
Portland St
Hill Street
King's Road
Fishpool Street
Mount
Pleasant
Offa Road
Abbey View Road
Old Oak Ct
Can Ct

FOLLY LANE
A4147
VERULAM ROAD
A5183
Victoria Playing Field
New England
Church Crs
Christchurch Ct
Worley Rd
Russell Clnc
Surg
Selby Av
Britton Av
Temperance St
Knights Orch
College St
Lower Dagnall St
College St
Queen St
Bowes Lyon Ms
Romeland
George St
Christophe Place
Romeland Hl

4
5
6
7

Kingsbury Watermill Museum & Waffle House
St Michael's Street
PH
M
St Michael's Manor Hotel
Ver Colne Valley Walk
The Lake
Ye Olde Fighting Cocks Inn
Abbey Mill End
Abbey Mill Lane
Monastery St
Orchard St
St Albans School
Abbey Gateway
Cathedral & Abbey Church of St Alban
Dean Moore Close
Orchard House La
Sumpter Yd
Abbey Primary School
Pondw Cl

Spencer St
Stapley
Upton Av
Adelaide St
Primary School
Drovers Way
St Peter's St
Waddon Rd
Cross St
Town Hall
Upr Dagnall St
French Row
Market Pl
HIGH ST
Clock Tower
Heritage Close Shopping Centre
Shopping Centre

Dalton Street
Bernard Street
Grange
Church Street
CATHERINE ST
Jubilee Centre
Works
Surgery
St Peter's St
Chime Sq
Surgery
Surg
Hall Place Close
Uni of Herts Faculty of Law
St Albans Museum
Alban Arena Cinema
PO
Law Courts
Surgery
Police Station
Crown Prosecution Service
Almshouses
Civic Centre
St Albans Principal Health Centre
Crown Court
Half Moon Mews
Westbourne Ms
The Maltings Shopping Centre
Maltings Arts Theatre
Bricket Rd
Marlborough Rd
A1081
Hart Road
Pageant Road
Albert Street
Sopwell Lane
Bardwell Road
Belmont Hill
Keyfield
Pearcess Walk
Old London Rd
Paxton Rd
Watson's Wlk
Hopkins Yd
Cottonmill
Old
LONDON ROAD
VICT
PO
A1081

Holywell Hill
A5183

514
A B 22 C D E
15

Sports Arena
Abbey View
Ver-Colne Valley Walk
Golf Course
Works
DeTany Ct
Albeny Ga
St Peters JMI School

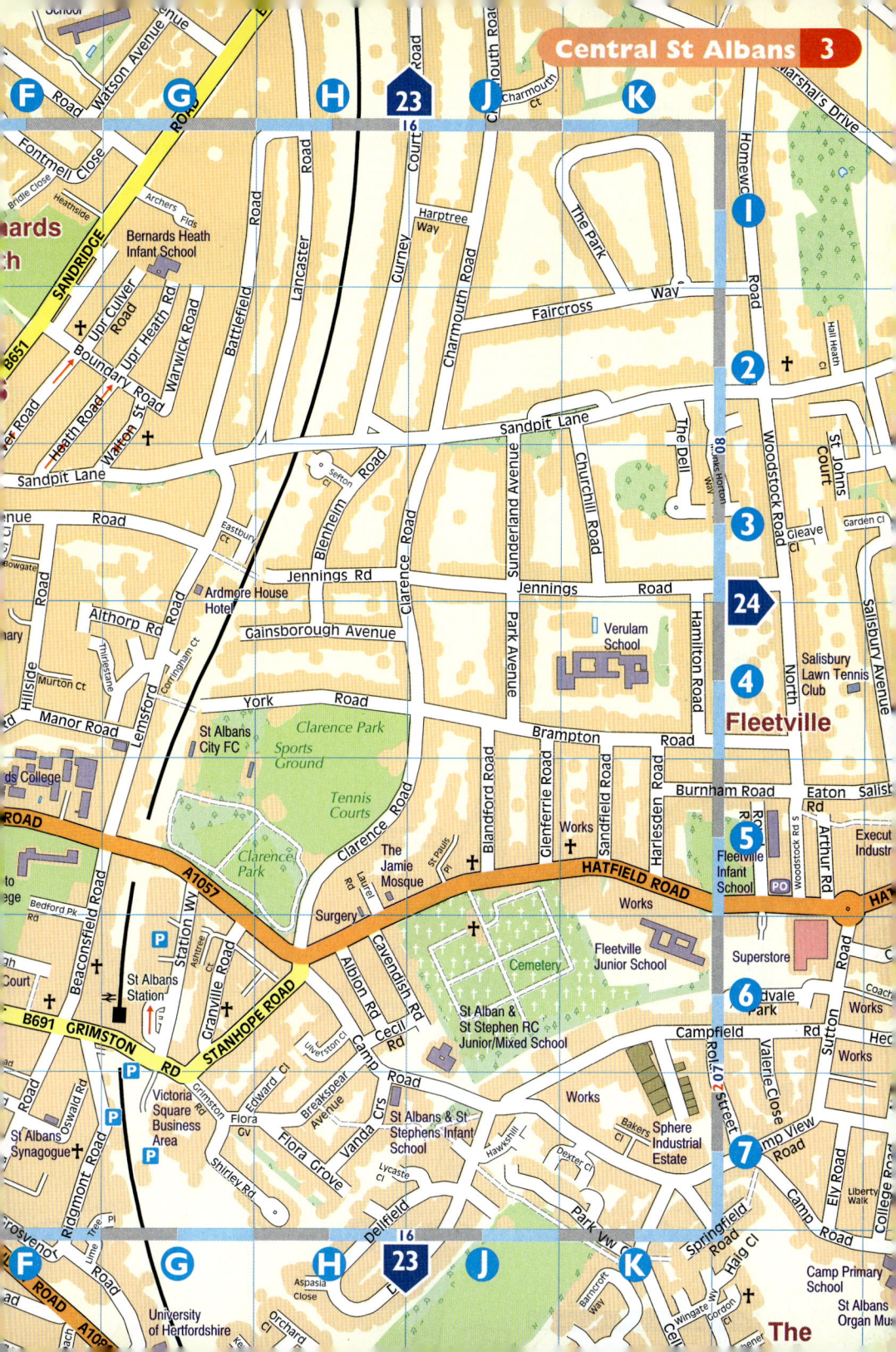

F G H 23 J K

I

2

3

24

4

Fleetville

5

6

7

F G H 23 J K

School

Fontmell Close

Watson Avenue

Bridle Close

Heathside

SANDRIDGE ROAD

B651

Bernards Heath Infant School

Archers Flds

Upr Culver Road

Boundary Road

Heath Road St

Watson St

Upr Heath Rd

Warwick Road

Battlefield Road

Lancaster Road

Gurney Court

Harptree Way

Charmouth Road

Charmouth Ct

The Park

Faircross Way

Homewc

Marshal's Drive

Hall Heath

Woodstock Road

St Johns Court

ards ch

ref Road

Sandpit Lane

Sandpit Lane

Sefton Cl

Eastbury Ct

Blenheim Road

Clarence Road

Sunderland Avenue

Churchill Road

The Dell

80 mus Morton Way

Gleave Cl

Garden Cl

3

Salisbury Avenue

enue

Road

Bowgate

Althorp Rd

Corringham Ct

Thirlestane

Murton Ct

Hillside

Lemsford Road

Ardmore House Hotel

Jennings Rd

Gainsborough Avenue

York Road

Jennings Road

Park Avenue

Hamilton Road

Verulam School

24

Salisbury Lawn Tennis Club

Salisbury Avenue

nary

Manor Road

St Albans City FC

Clarence Park Sports Ground

Tennis Courts

Brampton Road

Burnham Road

Eaton Rd

Salish

ds College

ROAD

A1057

Clarence Park

Clarence Road

The Jamie Mosque

St Pauls Pl

Laurel Rd

Blandford Road

Glenferrie Road

Works

Sandfield Road

Harlesden Road

Works

Fleetville Infant School

Woodstock Rd S

Arthur Rd

Execut Industr

Bedford Pk Rd

to ge

Beaconsfield Road

Station Wy

Asstree Rd

Granville Road

STANHOPE ROAD

Albion Rd

Surgery

Cavendish Rd

Cecil Rd

HATFIELD ROAD

Works

PO

5

Hat

B691 GRIMSTON RD

St Albans Station

P

Victoria Square Business Area

P

P

Oswald Rd

St Albans Synagogue

Ridgmont Road

Court

Grimston Rd

Edward Ct

Flora Gv

Shirley Rd

Breakspear Avenue

Flora Grove

Camp Road

Vanda Crs

Lycaste Cl

St Albans & St Stephens Infant School

Hawkshill

Dexter Cl

Cemetery

Fleetville Junior School

St Alban & St Stephen RC Junior/Mixed School

Works

Bakers Cl

Sphere Industrial Estate

Superstore

Campfield Road

Roll 2702 Street

dvale Park

Works

Rd

Works

Valerie Close

Camp Road

Sutton Rd

Hed

6

Liberty Walk

7

Grosvenor ROAD A109

Lime Tree Pl

Orchard

Aspasia Close

Delfield

23

Park Vw Gr

Barncroft Way

Springfield Road

Haig Cl

Wingate Wy

Gordon Cl

Camp View Road

Ely Road

College Road

Camp Primary School

St Albans Organ Mus

The

University of Hertfordshire

16

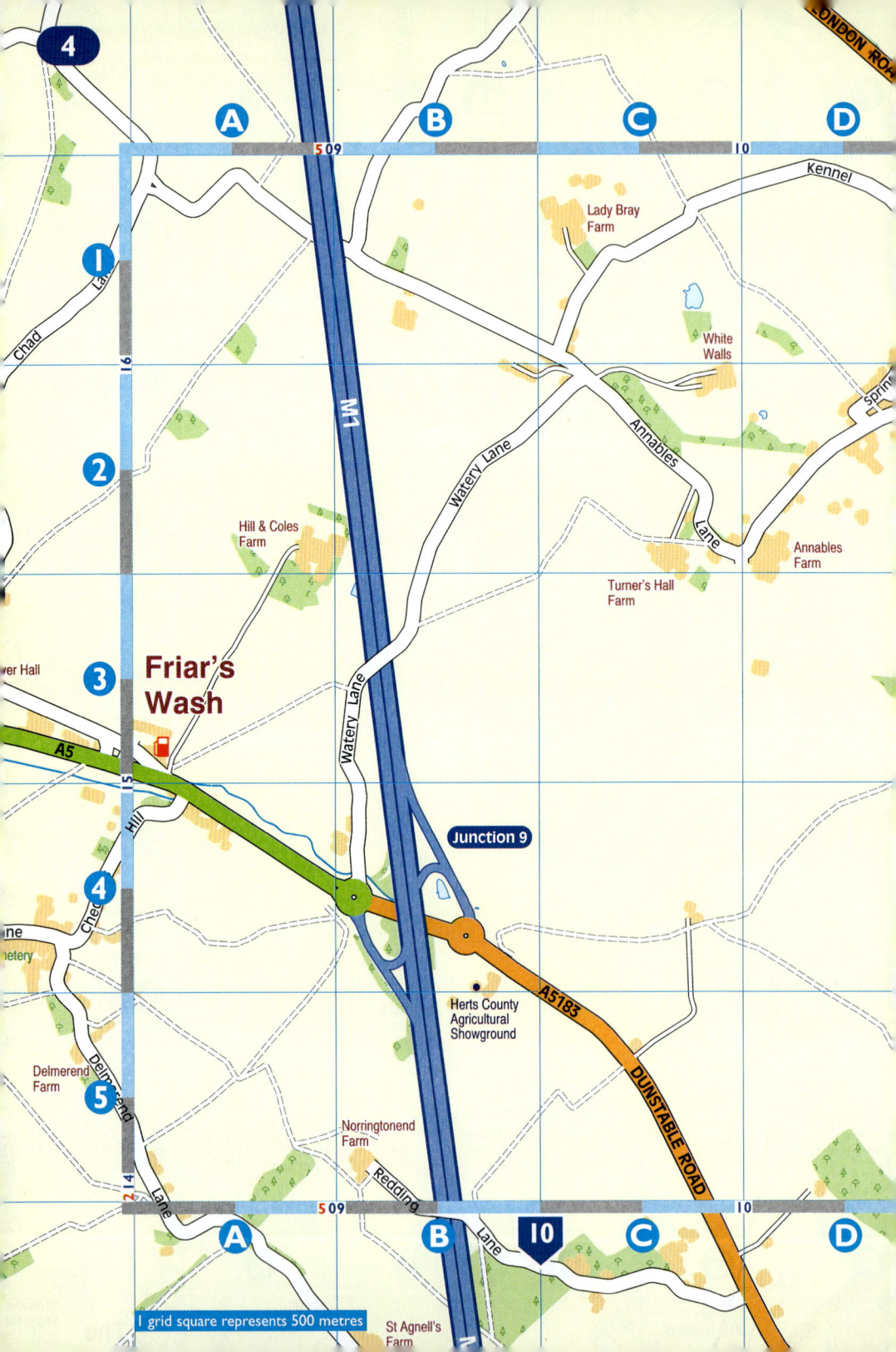

4

A 5 09 B C 10 D

I

Chad La...

M1

Kennel

Lady Bray Farm

White Walls

Sprin...

Annables Lane

2

Watery Lane

Hill & Coles Farm

Turner's Hall Farm

Annables Farm

3

...er Hall

Friar's Wash

A5

Hill...

Watery Lane

Junction 9

4

Ched...

...etery

...ne

Herts County Agricultural Showground

A5183

5

Delmerend Farm

Delmerend ...

2 14

Lane

Norringtonend Farm

Redding Lane

DUNSTABLE ROAD

A 5 09 B **10** C 10 D

St Agnell's Farm

LONDON ROA...

1 grid square represents 500 metres

E　　　F　　　G　　　H

11　　　　　　　　　12

**Kinsbourne
Green**

Thrales
End

Luton Road

† †

PO

The　Common

I

Bedfordshire County
Hertford County

Cooters End Lane

Amb

2

Derwent
Road Cl

Kinsbourne
Cl

Tintern Cl

The Close

The
Pleasance

K Crs

Prshr's

Vale Cl

Farm Av

Molescroft

Crpndr's Cl

Shphr Wy

Crosspaths

Creaxfield

Tuffnells

Tuffnells
Way

Ymn Av

Wood End
Hl

Wood End
School

Wood End Road

Ridge Avenue

Wells
Cl

Ridgewood Drive

Mayfield

High
Rd

Ridge'd Gdns

Luton Rd

A1081

LUTON RD

Woodlands

Roundwood Lane

Applewood

How
Field

Park Rise

Harp

Bloom

Asquit
Court
Scho

3

6

Ashley Gdns

Haslingden

Brackendale
Grove

Falconers Field

Roundwood Lane

Roundwood

Spnny

Roundwood Gdns

Park Rise

Park Mount

Hill

Park
End

Moreton Av

Moreton

MED

Kinsbourne Green Lane

Roundwood Lane

Faulkners
End Farm

Medlows

Park

Roundwood
Park School

Roundwood
Prim Sch

Newmans
Drive

4

Delgarth

Claygate Avenue

Pondwick
Rd

nders End La

Broadfields

Towns

Townsend
Lane

Barns Dene

Hartwell
Gardens

Townsend La

Maple
Road

Park Av North

Longcro

5

Redbourn
Golf Club

Park

Avenue

Townsend La

South

Orch

2　4

HARP

E　　　F　　　G　　　H

11　　　　　　　　　12

Golf Cou

II

Rothamsted Experimental
Station

A B C D

1

Bedfordshire County
Hertfordshire County

Thrales

End Road

River Lea or Lee

B653

LOWER

LUTON

B652

BOWER

HEATH

Cold Harb

2

A1081

LUTON ROAD

Cooters End Lane
Ambrose Lane
End Lane

The Kings School

Springfield Crs
Moorland Road
Riverford Cl
Westfield Drive
Rye Hl
Hyde
Coldharbour

Lea Industrial Estate

Riverside Estate

The Lea Primary School
Westfield Cemetery
Westfield Road
Maserfield Rd
Lindley Close

Allied Business Centre

Harpenden Hospital

Highfield Oval

Bloomfield Road
Hillside Road
Highfield Lane

St James' Rd
Lea Rd
Jameson Rd
Clarendon Rd

Oulton Rise
Wroxham Wy
Waveney Rd

3

5

Asquith Court School
Harpenden Rd
Park
Park Rise
Park Mount

Hollybush
Wordsworth Rd
Bryant Ct
Byron Cl
Ambrs La

Lane

Westfield Av
Dell Cl
Ox Fallows Green
Tennyson Road
Pigeonwick

Manland Primary School

Sir John Lawes School

Cross Way
West Way
Manland Way
Barton

4

Roundwood Prim Sch

Meadows
Roundwood Gdns
Park
Moreton
Moreton Av
Douglas Road
End

Newmans Drive
St Hildas School
Aplins Cl
Harpenden Health Cen
Townsend Road
Hitherfield Road
Lodge Gdns

Carlton Rd
Sun Lane
Bowers Wy

St Georges Sch Technology College

Harpenden Memorial Hosp

Surgery
Elliswick Lawn Tennis Club

Stewart Road
Sauncey Av
Grant Gdns
Elliswick Rd
Amberle Cl
Browning Rd

Dalkeith Rd

5

Clavgate Avenue
Barns Dene
Alders End
Broadfields
Townsend Lane
Roseberry Av
Salisbury Avenue

The Bourne
Kirkdale Road

AL5
Primary School
Avenue St
Nicholas
Leyton Green

High Street
Church St
A1081
Leyton Rd
Vaughan

Surgery
Oaklands Coll
Milton Rd

Station Rd

STATION ROAD

Overstone Road
Cowper Rd
Granary Lane
Shakespeare Rd
Spenser Rd
Gilpin Rd
Crabtree Rd

Hartwell Gardens
Park Av North
Longcroft Av
Maple Rd
Kirkwick Avenue
Orchard
South
Park Av
Amenbury La
Hay La

Town Hall

HARPENDEN

Harpenden Swimming Pool

PO
Arden
Harpenden Station

Harpenden Station
Southdown Road

Copper Beeches

A B C **12** C D

Harpenden Sports Centre

Harpenden Hotel

St Dominic RC Primary School

Crabtree
Fairmead
Topstreet
Meadow
Crast

Sir Joseph's Walk

1 grid square represents 500 metres

Lane

wer Heath

E F G H

15 16

The Slype

Wood

Turners
Hall Farm

I

Sauncey

Common Lane

Marshalls Heath Lane

16

*Sauncey
Wood*

Sauncey
Wood

2

Whitings Cl

ford Hill

Milford Hl

**Mackerye
End**

Sauncey
Wood
Prim School

Fulmore Cl

field Av

Holcroft Rd

Finley Rd

Milford Hill

**Marshalls
Heath**

Tallents Crs

Batford
Road

Batford

**Lea
Valley**

3

8

ry Rd

Lwr Lt Rd

Valley Rd

Manor Road

Castle Rd

Marshalls
Way

Lwr Luton Rd

5

us La

Marquis Lane

Marquis Cl

Lea Valley Walk

Cherry Tree Dr

Leasey Dell

4

venue

Lane

Glemsford Dr

Weybourne Cl

Holly Walk

Altwood

Tyler's Cl

Lea Valley Walk

LOWER LUTON ROA

Folly Fields

Av

DW

P Cl

Eng

Leasey Bridge

5

Brampton

The Cleave

Wn Cl

Waldegrave Pk

Ashwell Pk

Piggottshill

Lane

Golf Course

Leasey Bridge Lane

Leasey Bridge Lane

ickbury Crs

High Beeches
Prim Sch

Aldwickbury Park
Golf Club

E

Alzey

Gdns

F

Hilltop Wk

13

Aldwickbury
School

G

Nheathampstead Road

H

Poynings Close

Lane

Wheathampstead Rd

Wheathampstead

g Buflers

Harpenden

15 16

214

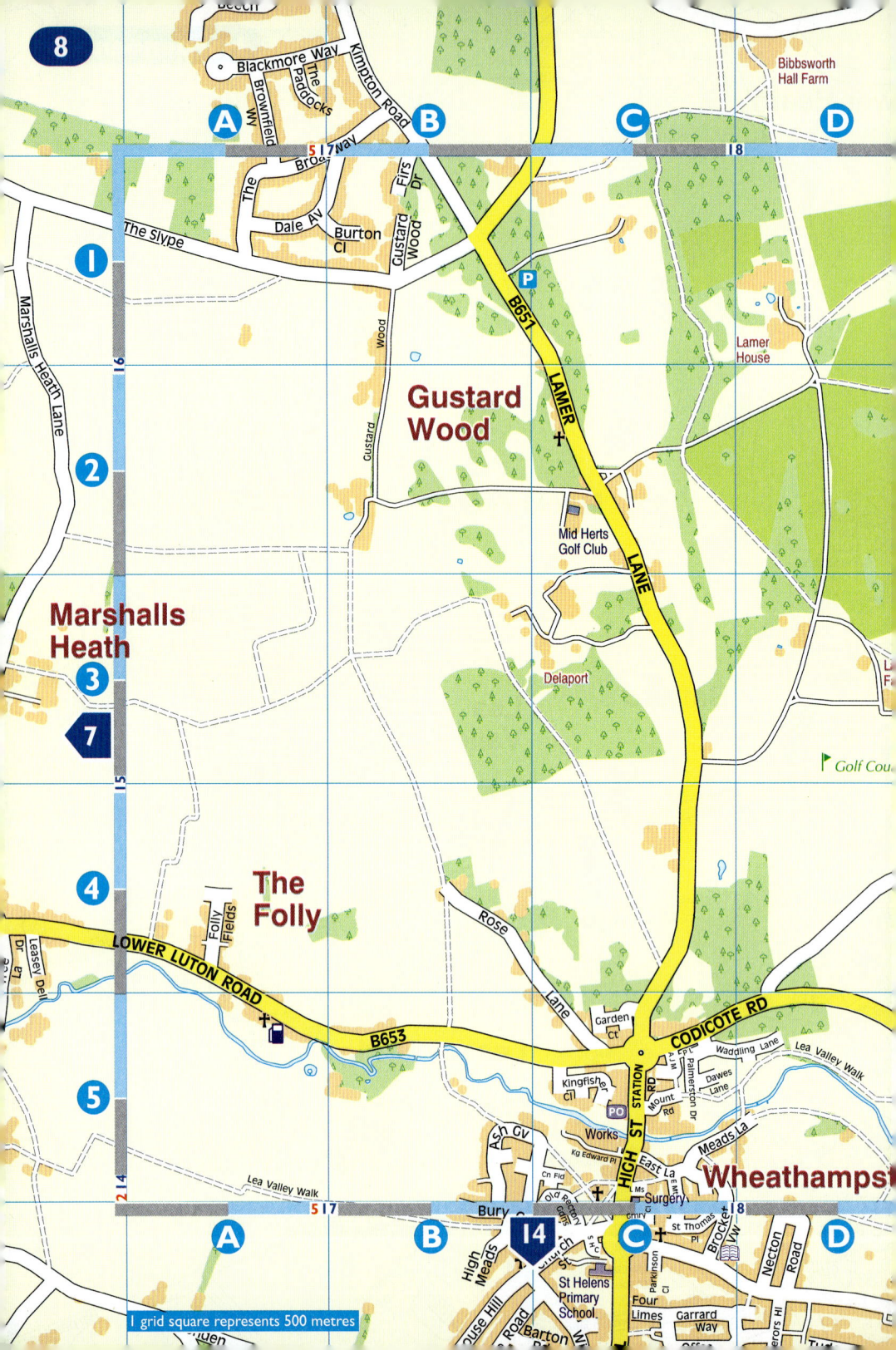

8

Blackmore Way

Brownfield Wy

The Paddocks

Kimpton Road

Bibbsworth
Hall Farm

A   B   C   D

5 17 Way   18

The Slype

The Broad Wy

Dale Av

Burton Cl

Firs Dr

Gustard Wood

P

B651

Lamer
House

1

16

Marshalls Heath Lane

Gustard

Wood

Gustard

Gustard
Wood

LAMER

2

Mid Herts
Golf Club

LANE

Marshalls
Heath

Delaport

3

15

7

Golf Cou

4

The
Folly

Folly Fields

Rose Lane

Leasey Del Dr

LOWER LUTON ROAD

CODICOTE RD

Waddling Lane

Lea Valley Walk

B653

Garden
Ct

Palmerston Dr

Dawes
Lane

Meads La

5

Kingfisher
Cl

PO

HIGH ST

STATION RD

Mount
Rd

Works

Ash Gv

Kg Edward Pl

East La

Surgery

Wheathamps

Lea Valley Walk

2 14

5 17   18

A   B   14   C   D

High Meads

Bury

Church

St Helens
Primary
School

Old Rectory
Gdns

Cn Fld

St Ms

st Thomas
Pl

Parkinson Cl

Brocket Vw

Necton
Road

Four
Limes

Garrard
Way

Mrors HI

House Hill Road

Barton Rd

1 grid square represents 500 metres

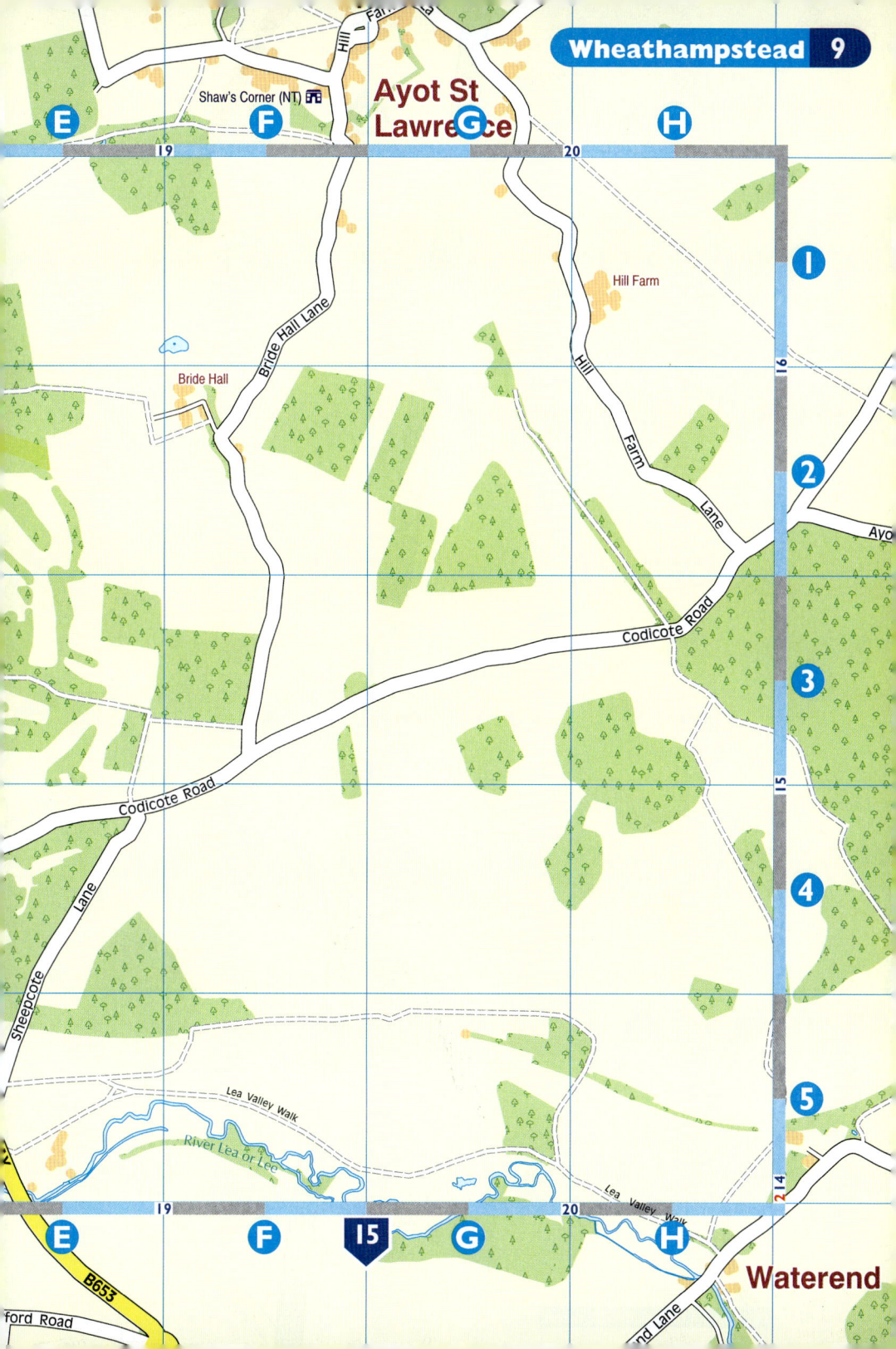

E F **Ayot St** G H
Lawrence

Shaw's Corner (NT)

I

19 20

Hill Farm

16

Bride Hall Lane

Bride Hall

Hill Farm Lane

2

Ayo

Codicote Road

3

15

Codicote Road

4

Sheepcote Lane

5

Lea Valley Walk

River Lea or Lee

14

19 20

E F **15** G H

Lea Valley Walk

Waterend

B653

ford Road

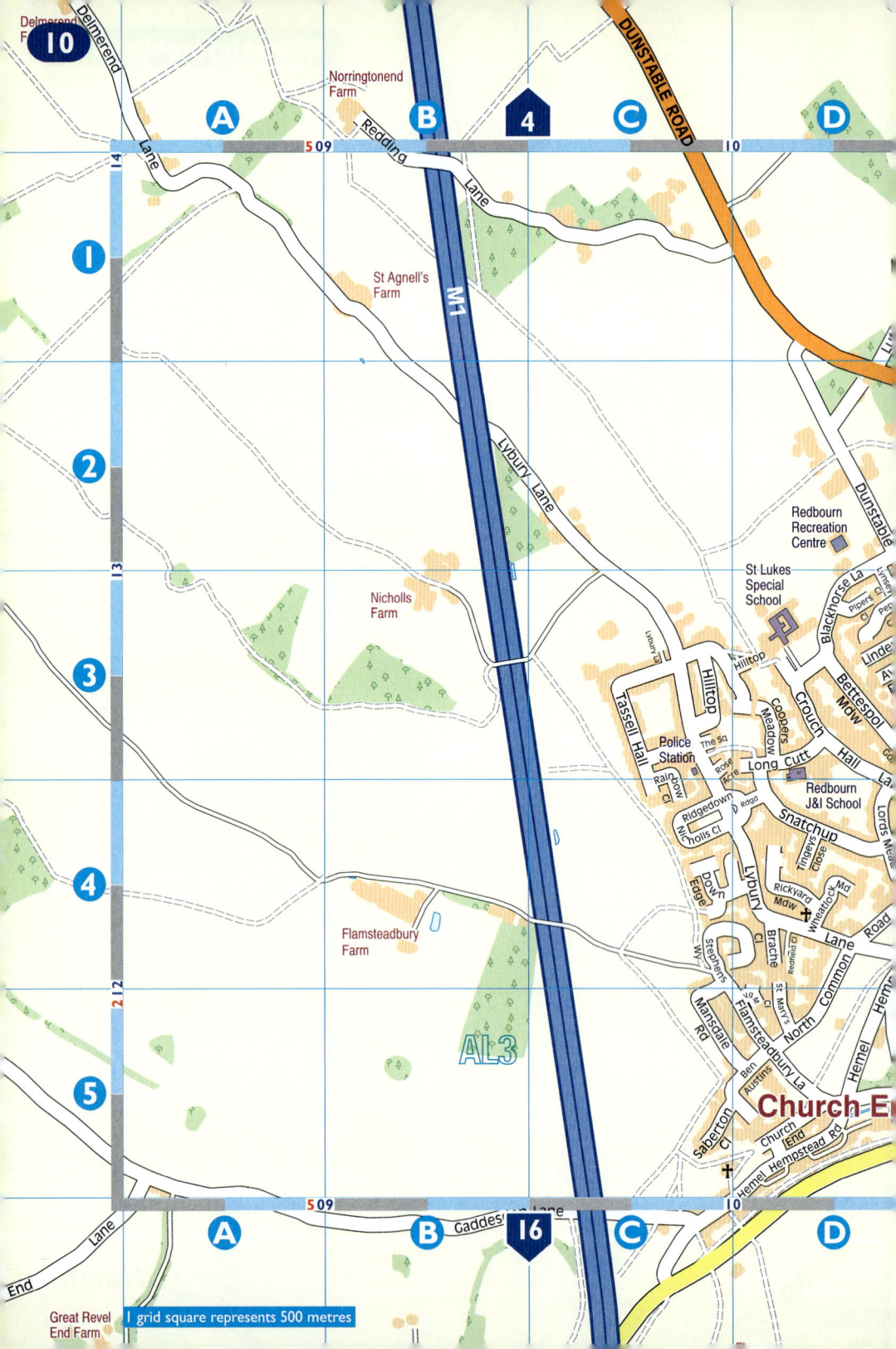

Delmerend
F

A

B

4

C

D

Norringtonend
Farm

Redding

Lane

DUNSTABLE ROAD

509

14

1

St Agnell's
Farm

M1

10

2

13

Lybury Lane

Redbourn
Recreation
Centre

St Lukes
Special
School

Blackhorse La

Dunstable

Pipers

Cl

Linde

3

Nicholls
Farm

Tassell Hall

Police
Station

The Sq

Rose
Acre

Hilltop

Hilltop

Coopers
Meadow

Crouch

Bettespol
Mdw

Hall

Long Cutt

Redbourn
J&I School

Snatchup

Lords Mead

4

12

Rain Bow

Ridgedown

Nicholls Cl

Down
Edge

Lybury

Tingeys
Close

Wheatlock
Mdw

Rickyard
Mdw

Lane

North

Common

Road

Hemel

5

Flamsteadbury
Farm

AL3

Mansdale
Rd

Stephens
Wy

Brache

St Mary's

Ben
Austins

Flamsteadbury La

Redbarm

Saberton
Cl

Church
End

Hemel Hempstead Rd

Church E

509

509

10

A

B

16

C

D

Gaddesden Lane

End
Lane

Great Revel
End Farm

1 grid square represents 500 metres

E | Redbourn Golf Club

F

5

G

H

Golf Course

Rothamsted Experimental Station

I

83

2

13

edbourn

Lane

B487

REDBOURN

3

12

Scout Farm

Harpenden RUFC

Harpenden

Ver Rd

Flint Copse

Appletree Grove

Cumberland Dr

Hammond End Lane

Golf Course

Harpe Golf C

High St

Crown St

Hrd Crown St

Bessett

PO

Hawkes Dr

Miller Cl

Waterend

La

The T Mews

Phizom

The Ruins

Monks Cl

Redbourn Industrial Centre

Health Cen

4

Fish St

Fs St F

Hammonds End Farm

The Park

A5183

2 12

The Park

The

Hammonds

Chequer La

5

Ver-Colne Valley Walk

ST ALBANS ROAD

The Elms

E

F

17

G

H

A51

HARPENDEN

12

Grid references: A B C D — rows I, 1, 11, 2, 3, 4, 5

Harpenden Gardens · Park Av · Kirkwick Avenue · Rothamsted · South · Orchard Av · Nicholas · Avenue St · The Dr · Glenbury · Hay La · La Lane · Town Hall · St A Av · Leyton Green · Leyton Rd · Vaughan Rd · Coll · Pits · Copper Beeches · Shakespeare Rd · Milton · Globe Rd · Lane · Road · Road · Overstone Rd

Park Avenue · **HARPENDEN** · Avenue St · Harpenden Swimming Pool · 5 13 · **6** · Arden Gv · Southdown Road · Harpenden Station · PO · Spenser Rd · Milton Rd · Gn · Dublin

A · **B** · **C** · **D**

Harpenden Sports Centre · Bull Rd · Harpenden House Hotel · Southdown Road · Furzedown · Aysgarth Cl · Linden · St Dominic RC Primary School · Crabtree · Fairmead Av · Topstreet · Wa

I

Sir Joseph's Walk · Meadow Wk · Southdown Industrial Estate · Barnfield Rd · Churchf · Marlborough Pk · Crons Wk

West Common · A1081 · Bowling · Heath Cl · Queens Rd · Road · St Johns Rd · PO · Southdown Rd · Vallance · Colen

2

W Common · Redcote La · Greyfriars La · Flowton Gv · Walkers · Harpenden Common · Cravells · Eastmoor Park · Eastmoor Pk · Little La

Hatching Green

Harpenden Common

REDBOURN LANE · Harpenden RUFC · **3** · **11** · Hatching Green Cl · High Elms · The Warren · W Common · W C · Harpenden Common Golf Club · Limbrick Road · Grange Ct · Beech Cl

Golf Course · Hammond End Lane · Oakhurst Avenue · Oakfield Road · Dellcroft Way · West Common Way · W Comm Cl · West Common Gv · Golf Course · Cross Lane

4

Hammonds End Farm · Harpenden Golf Club · Fairway Close · Oakwood Drive · Oakwood Cl · Oakfield Rd · Garden Cl · Barlings Rd · The Chowns · Collens Rd · Burywick

Hammonds Hill · Oak Way · Winton Av · Wheatfield Rd · The Uplands · Hawsley Rd · Netherfield Rd

5

Hammondswick · The Deenings · Penny Croft · Prospect Lane · Beesonend Farm · Childwick Hall · A1081 · Hart

Beesonend Lane

A · **B** · **18** · **C** · **D**

5 13 · 14

Hedge's Farm

I grid square represents 500 metres

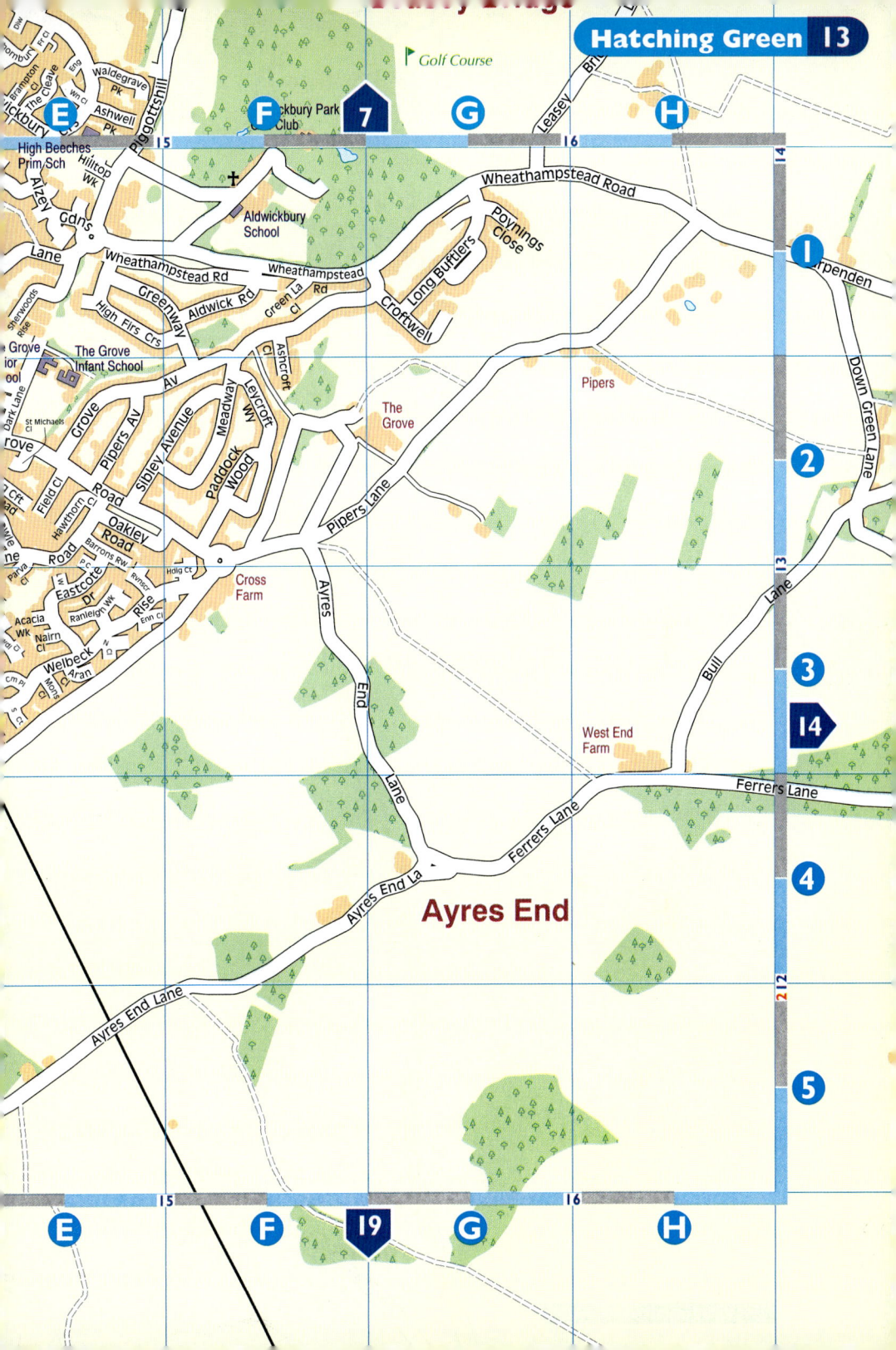

Golf Course

E

F Aldwickbury Park Club 7

G

H

Leasey

I Harpenden

Wheathampstead Road

Poynings Close

Long Butlers

High Beeches Prim Sch

Hilltop Wk

Alzey Gdns

Aldwickbury School

Wheathampstead Rd

Wheathampstead Rd

Greenway

Aldwick Rd

Green La

Croftwell

High Firs Crs

Cl

Pipers

Sherwoods Rise

Ashcroft

The Grove

The Grove Infant School

Grove

Av

Levcroft Wy

Meadway

Paddock Wood

Pipers Av

Sibley Avenue

The Grove

St Michaels Cl

Dark Lane

Pipers Lane

Field Cl

Hawthorn Cl

Grove Road

Oakley Road

Barrons Rw

Haig Ct

Cross Farm

Ayres End Lane

Down Green Lane

1

2

Bull Lane

3

West End Farm

14

Eastcote Dr

Ranelegh Wk

Rise

Enn Cl

Welbeck

Aran

Acacia Wk

Nairn Cl

Ferrers Lane

Ferrers Lane

4

212

Ayres End

Ayres End Lane

5

14

Lea Valley Way 5 17 B C 8 D Wheathampst

14

Kingfisher Cl
ST STATION
Dawes Lane
Mount Rd
Walk
PO
Works
Kg Edward Pl
Ash GV
Meads La

St La
Surgery
St Thomas
Pl
Brocket Vw
Necton Road
18

Bury Green
Old Rectory Gdns
St Helens Primary School
Four Limes
Parkinson
Garrard Way
Conquerors Hl
Tudor Rd
Battleview

1

Harpenden
Road

High Meads
Brewhouse Hill
Barton Rd
Wick
Offas Way
Caesars
Saxon Road
Nurseries Rd
S Cl

Lattimore Road
Church St
Road

2

Down Green Lane
Amwell
Butterfield
High Ash Rd
Lane
Road
Maltings Dr
Av
Beech Hyde Primary School
Wright
HS Cl
Davys Cl
Allen
Hewitt
Hill Dyke Rd
Vale Court
Beech Crs

Amwell

Lane

3

Bull
13

Nomansland

B651

Ferrers Lane

Nomansland Common
Ferrers Lane

Dyke Lane
Beech Farm

4

2 12
Ferrers
Lane
Nomansland Farm

5

Hillend Farm

5 17 A B 20 C D 18

Coleman Green
Lane

1 grid square represents 500 metres

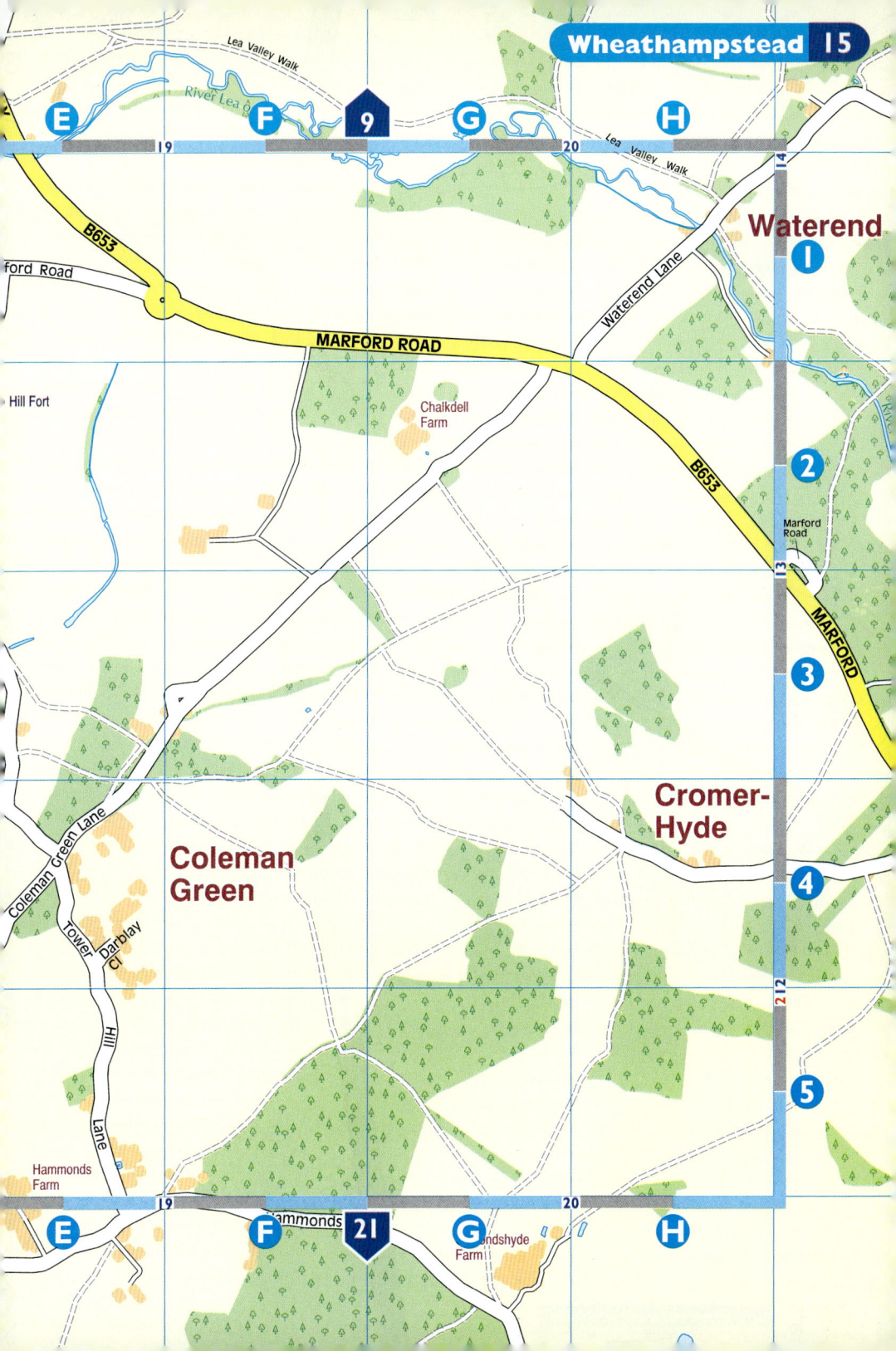

E

F

9

G

H

19

20

Lea Valley Walk

Lea Valley Walk

River Lea

14

B653

ford Road

MARFORD ROAD

Waterend Lane

Waterend

I

Hill Fort

Chalkdell
Farm

B653

2

Marford
Road

13

3

MARFORD

**Cromer-
Hyde**

Coleman Green Lane

**Coleman
Green**

Tower

Darblay
Ct

4

Hill

Lane

212

5

Hammonds
Farm

E

19

F

Hammonds

21

G

ndshyde
Farm

H

20

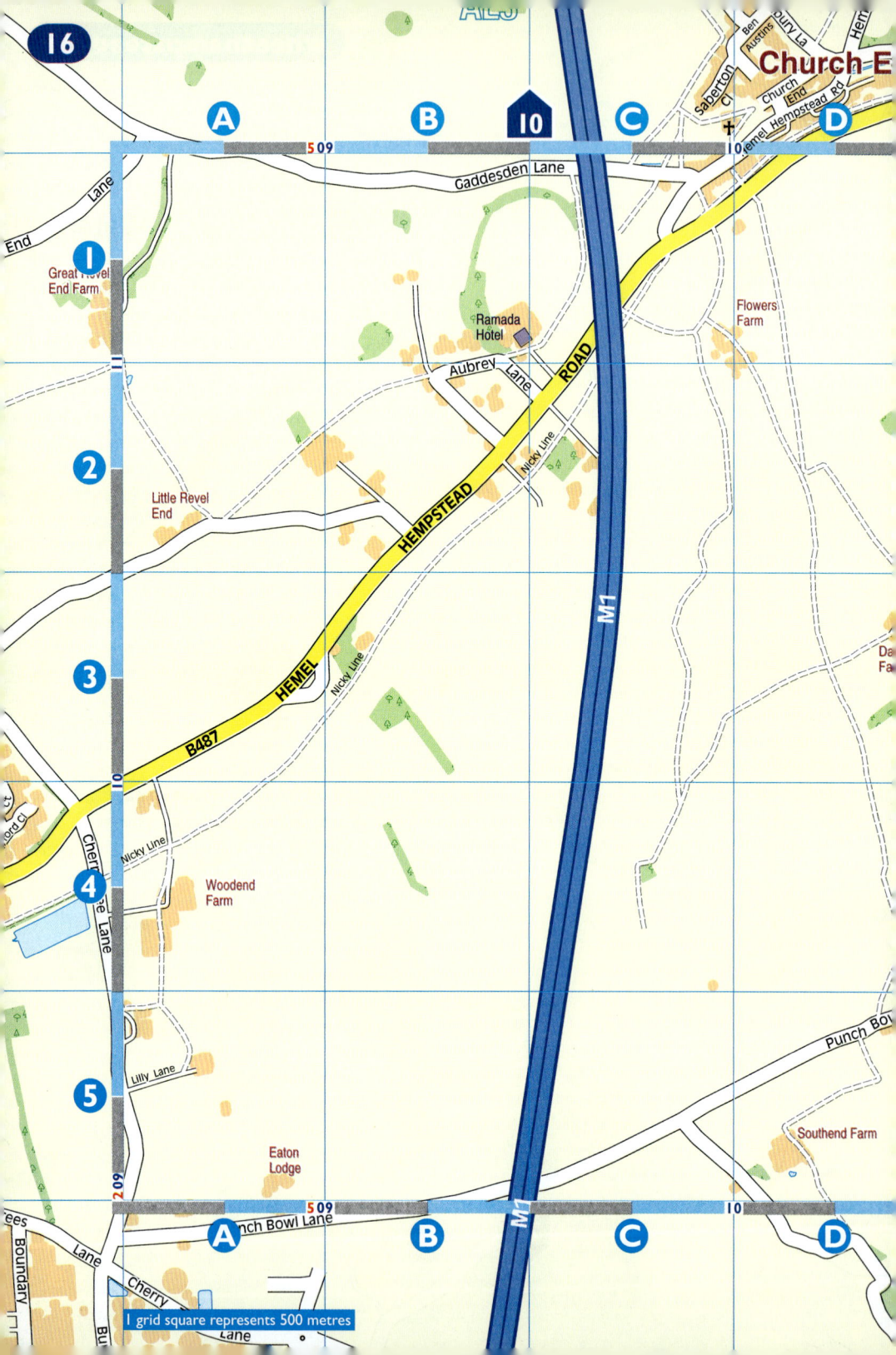

16

A   **B**   10   C   **Church E**

5 09

Gaddesden Lane

Ben Austins
bury La
Henr
Saberton Cl
Church End
Hemel Hempstead Rd
D

Flowers Farm

1

Great Revel End Farm

Ramada Hotel

Aubrey Lane

ROAD

2

Little Revel End

Nicky Line

HEMPSTEAD

Nicky Line

Da Fa

3

HEMEL

Nicky Line

B487

M1

Cherry

ord Cl

Nicky Line

4

Woodend Farm

Punch Bo

5

Lilly Lane

Eaton Lodge

Southend Farm

2 09

rees

Boundary

Lane

Cherry

5 09

A   nch Bowl Lane   **B**   M1   C   10   **D**

Bu

Lane

1 grid square represents 500 metres

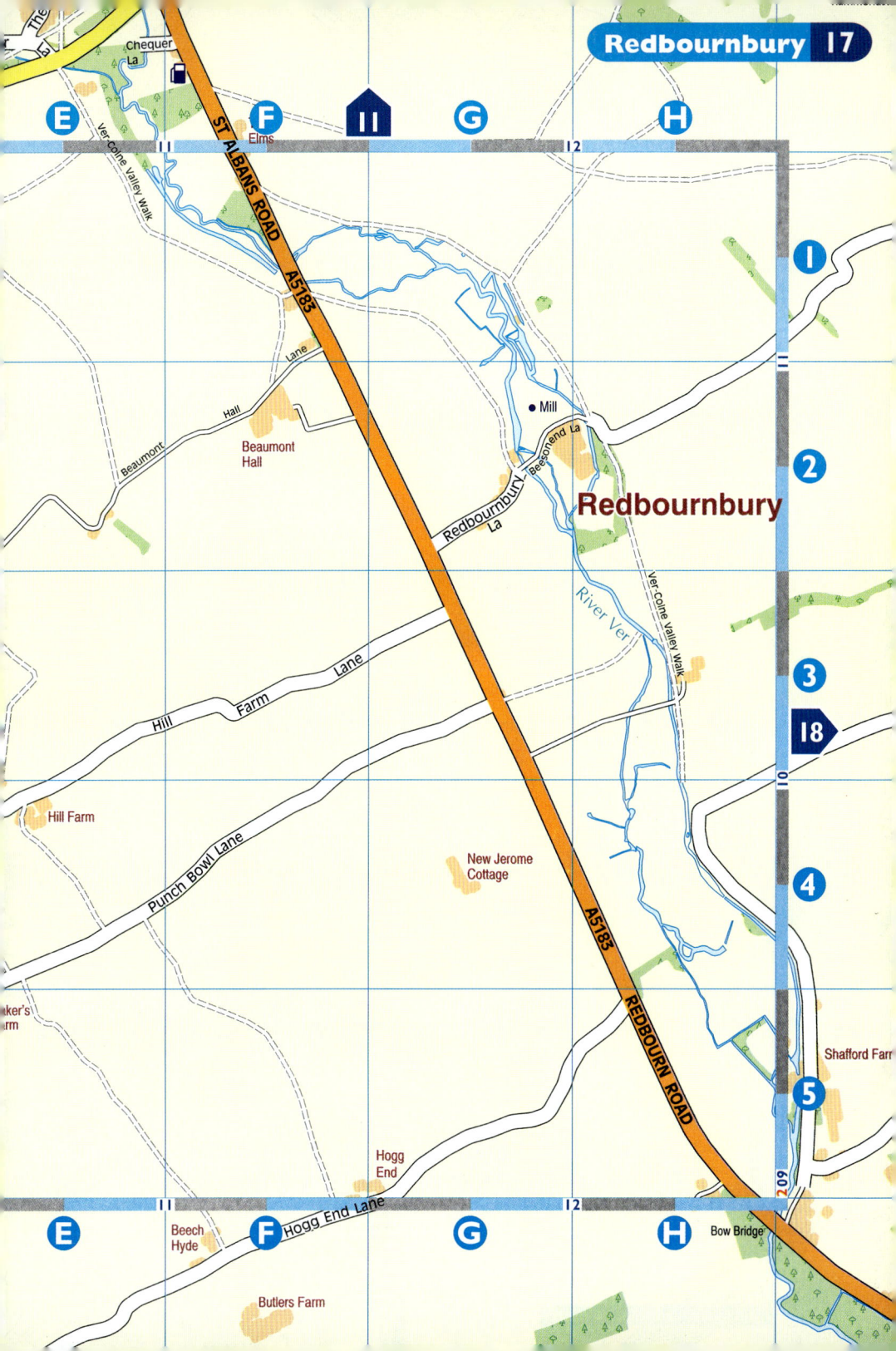

Redbournbury 17

E F G H

Chequer La

ST ALBANS ROAD A5183

Elms

Ver-Colne Valley Walk

I

Lane

Hall

Beaumont

Beaumont Hall

Mill

2

Redbournbury La

Beesonend La

Redbournbury

River Ver

Ver-Colne Valley Walk

Hill Farm Lane

3

18

Hill Farm

Punch Bowl Lane

New Jerome Cottage

4

A5183 REDBOURN ROAD

Shafford Farm

5

209

Hogg End

Beech Hyde

Hogg End Lane

Bow Bridge

Butlers Farm

E F G H

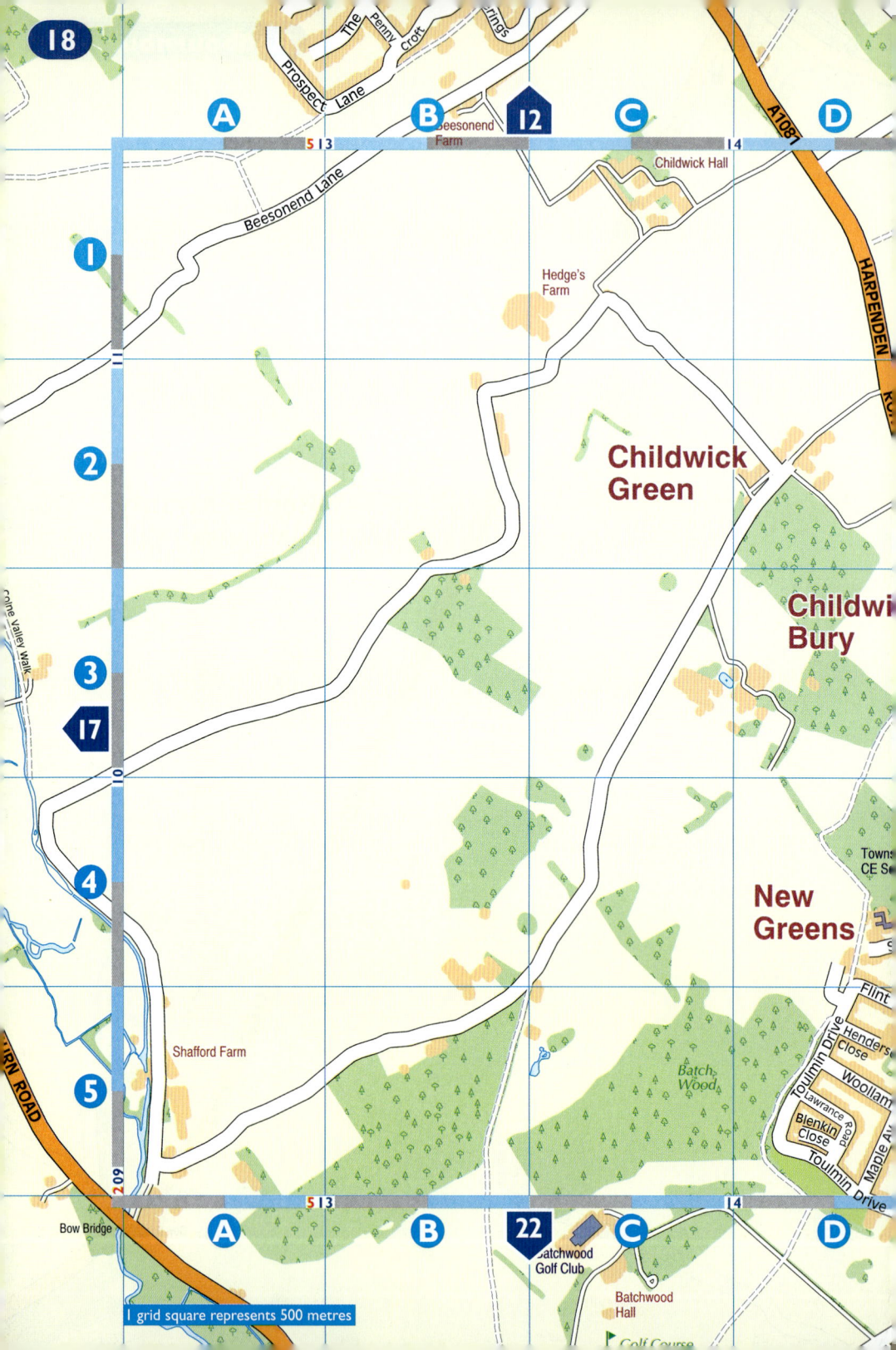

18

A B 12 C D

Prospect Lane
The Penny Croft
Beesonend Farm
Childwick Hall
A1081
HARPENDEN

Beesonend Lane

1

Hedge's Farm

RIVER

2

Childwick Green

Colne Valley Walk

Childwick Bury

3

17

New Greens

Towns... CE S...

4

Flint
Henders... Close
Toulmin Drive
Woollam
Lawrance Road
Maple Av...
Blenkin Close

Shafford Farm

Batch Wood

5

...RN ROAD

209

A B 22 C D

Bow Bridge
Batchwood Golf Club
Batchwood Hall

Golf Course

I grid square represents 500 metres

E F **13** G H

15 16

I

2

Sandridgebur

Sandridge
Club & Spor

3

20

Cheapside
Farm

Sandridgebury

Reynol
Crescent

St Heliers Rd

4

Sandr

Lane

Cavan

Petersfield

Long
Spring

Porters Wood

The Gryphon
Industrial Park

Wheatfields
J&I School

Sandringh
School

Blundell Cl

Carnegie Road

Partridge Road

New Greens Avenue

ROAD

HARPENDEN

Sandridgebury

St Albans
Girls School

Darwin
Close

Valley

Road

Soothouse
Spring

Canberra Cl

Sandridge
Gate Business
Centre

Melbourne
Cl

Sandringham
Crs

Bishop's

Breckon Field Cl

Runcie Cl

5

Oaks

Gilsted
Ct

Nicholas
Close

Stags
School

Tudor
Rd

Farriday
Cl

Ellis Flds

L Porters
Field

Firbank
Rd

Hobart
Walk

ST

ALBANS

Dean's
Gdns

Marten
Gate

Furse Av

Slimmons Dr

The Ridgeway

Pondfield
Crs

Kingshill Avenue

Queens

epton
reen
cis

Therfield
Rd

Drive

Batchwood
Gardens

Batchwood
School

A1081

Harpenden Rd

Ellis Flds

Beech Bottom

Sheppards

Seymou

Beech

Marshall Avenue

Bernards
Heath Junior
School

23

PO

B651

Chalkdell Flds

Dymoke
Gn

Ronsons
Way

ROAD

Marshal's

Wick Lane

Marshal's

Marshalswick

E F **23** G H

15

A **B** **14** **C** **D**

5 17 18

I

Hillend Farm

Coleman Green Lane

2

Langley
Spencer Pl
Sandridgebury Lane
Shortfield Cl
Grove
Lyndon Md
Sandridge School
Church Cl
Sandridge Youth Club & Sports Centre
St Leonards Crs
House Lane
Woodcockhill

3

19

Highfield Rd
Bus Cen
Gibbons
Anson

Sandridge

Jersey La

HIGH STREET
B651
Reynolds Crescent

4

ROAD B651
St Heliers Rd

Wendover Cl
Pirton Cl
Belsize Cl
Highview Gdns
Cromwell Close
Nashe's Farm
Lincoln's
Larkswood Rd
Sandringham Crescent
Wilstone Dr
Langham
Chancery Cl
Holborn

AL4

Chiltern Road
Mayfair
Portman Cl
Regent
Sandringham Crescent

5

Slimmons Dr
Wheatfields J&I School
Malvern Cl
Chiltern Rd
Windmill Av
Windmill Av
Berkeley Close
Richmond walk
Craiglands
Sandringham School
Downs Road
Ridgeway
Skys Wd Road
Bentsley Close
Tewin Close
The Ridgeway
PO
Harvest Ct
Beverley Gdns
Ripon Wy
Bishop's Close
Furse Av
Pondfield Crs
Avenue
Evans Grove
Chandlers Rd
The Larches
Milford
Cheriton Cl
Stanton Cl
Marten
Marshal's

A **B** **24** **C** **D**

5 17 18

Kingshill Avenue
Queens Crs
Sherwood
Hazelmere
Skyswood JMI Sch
Blackthorn
Meadow
House Lane
Kingsmead
Oak Far

Marshalswick

Wycombe
St John Fisher RC Primary School
Woodfield Wy
Middlefield Wy
Briar Road
Villers
The
Levs
Springwood Walk

I grid square represents 500 metres

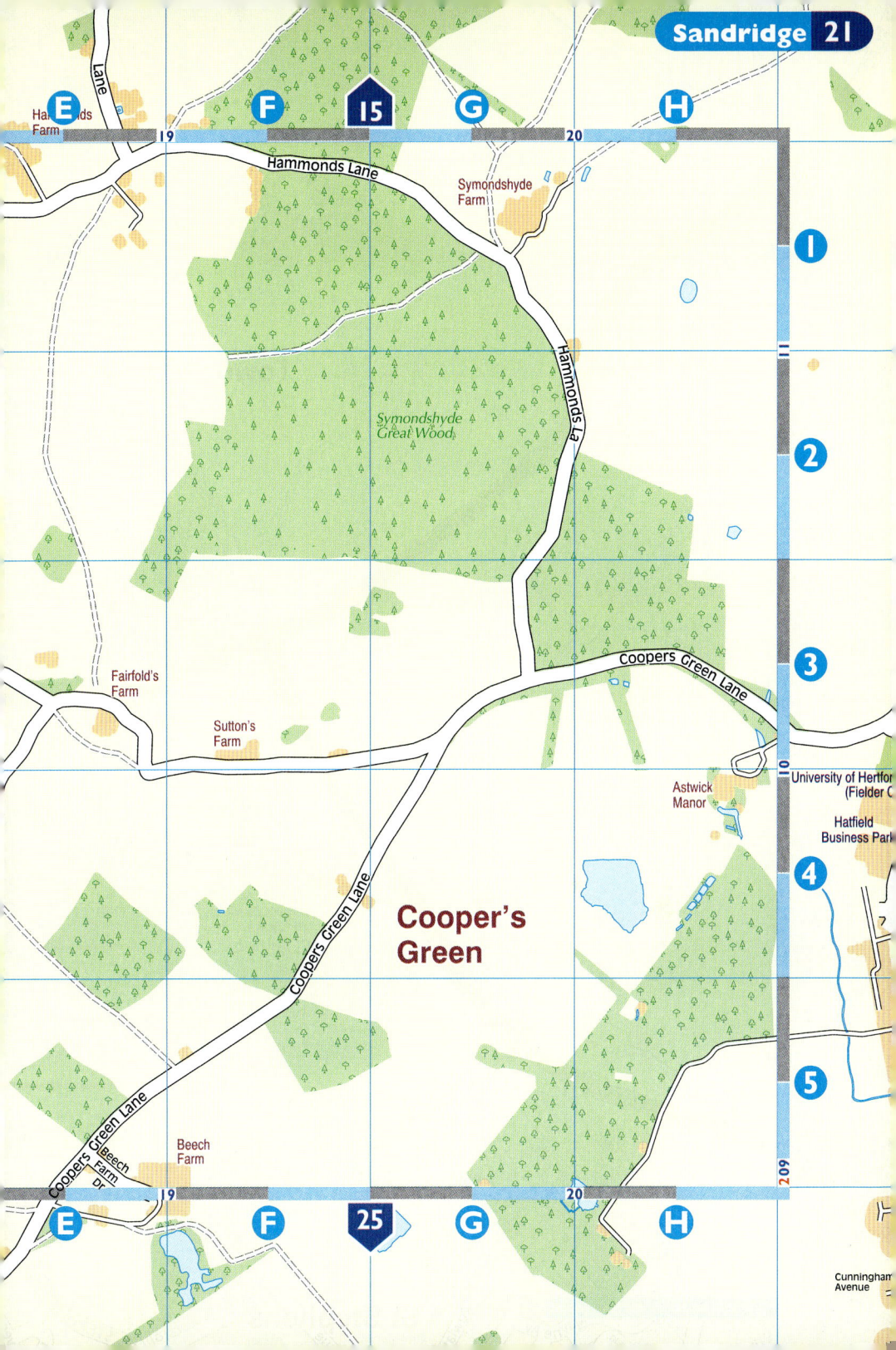

E
F
15
G
H

Hammonds Lane

Ha...ds Farm
19
20

Symondshyde Farm

Symondshyde Great Wood

Hammonds La

I

2

Coopers Green Lane

3

Fairfold's Farm

Sutton's Farm

Astwick Manor

University of Hertfor (Fielder C

Hatfield Business Park

4

Cooper's Green

Coopers Green Lane

Coopers Green Lane

5

Coopers Green Farm Dr

Beech Farm

E
F
25
G
H

209

Cunningham Avenue

A B 18 C D

5 13 14

I

Bow Bridge

Maynes Farm

2

River Ver

3

4

5

ROAD

09

08

2 07

REDBOURN ROAD A5183

HEMEL HEMPSTEAD ROAD

BLUEHOUSE HILL

HEMEL Hempstead Rd

ROAD A4147

Batch Wood

Batchwood Golf Club

Batchwood Hall

Golf Course

Townsend

Ladies Grove

Ladies Link

Ladies Grove

Ladies Grove

White Hedge Dr

View Rd

Everlasting Lane

Batchwood Drive

Downedge

Dormie Close

Waverley

Lavender Crs

Everlasting Road

Coughlan Rd

St Albans City Hospital

Temple

Artisan Crs

Wells

Artisan Crs

Thorns Street

VERULAM ROAD

FOLLY LANE A5183

Camlet Wy

Camlet Way

Frith Rd

Branch Rd

Oysterfields

Playing Field

Rec Gnd

St Michaels Prim Sch

Prae Cl

M

PH

Kingsbury

St Michael's St

Museum

Mount Pleasant

King's Rd

Portland Street

Hill St

New England St

Old Lw

Roman Theatre of Verulamium

Watermill Museum & Waffle House

Museum

Fishpool St

Abbey Vw Rd

Ver Rd

Old Ct

Rom

Grebe House Wildlife Centre & Gardens

St Michael's Manor Hotel

The Lake

Street

Abbey Gateway

St Albans School

Abbey Orchard St

Abbey Mill Lane

Verulamium Park

Ye Olde Fighting Cocks Inn

Abbey Mi End

Sports Arena

Golf Course

Abbey View Golf Club

P

Leisure Centre

P

Parklands Dr

Mayne Av

King

The Ramparts

Harry

Bedmond

Mayne Avenue

Lindum Pl

Augustus

Claudian

Antonine Ca

Ermine Av

Claudian

Prae Wood Prim Sch

Corinium

Close

Dubrae Close

Westfields

Flavian

Lindum

Mayne Av

Rowlatt

Lane

Cardinal Gv

Kingsgate

ST STEPHEN'S HL

A B 26 C D

5 13 14

St Stephens

E F 19 G H

Partridge Road
Gins School
Darwin Close
Soothn Spring
Sandridge Gate Business Centre
Canberra Cl
Dean's Gdns
School
The Ridgeway
Pondfield Crs
Kingshill Avenue
Queens

Oaks
Avenue
Stags School
Friday
Ellis Flds
Melbourne Rd
Fir bank RD
Hobart Walk
ST
Chalkdell Flds
Furse Av
Simmons Dr
Close
Saint

Nicholas Close
Tudor
Old Harpenden Rd
Beech
Marshall Avenue
Marshalswick Lane
Marshal's Drive
Homewood
Marshalswick
Hall Heath Close
Marsh

Avenue
Ellis Flds
Road
Bernards Heath Junior School
Road
Road
Road

Drive
Batchwood Gardens
Batchwood School
Beech Bottom
Garden Fields JMI School
Seymour
Watson Avenue
Charmouth Ct
The Park
Faircross Way

Acre
Heathlands Special School
Heathlands Dr
Fontmell Cl
Bridle Cl
Archers Flds
Bernards Heath Infant School
Harptree Way
Charmouth

2
Bernards Heath
SANDRIDGE ROAD
STONECROSS
Heathside
Boundary Rd
Upr Culver Rd
Upr Heath
Warwick Rd
Battlefield Road
Lancaster Road
Gurney Court
Churchill Rd
The Dell
Sandpit

May Drive
Edmund Beaufort Dr
Heath Farm Lane
Limes
Spencer Gate
Culver Rd
Heath
Waldes Rd
Sandpit Lane
Blenheim Rd
ST ALBANS
Sunderland Avenue
Woodstock Road N
Cleave

Pegasus
Palfrey Cl
Cricketers
A1081
Townsend
Sch
Avenue Road
Jennings Road
Jennings
Park Av
Verulam School
Hamilton Rd

Carlisle Av
Grange St
Surgery
Spencer
Bowgate
Ramsey Ldg Ct
Maple Primary School
Althorp Road
Murton Ct
Ardmore House Hotel
Gainsborough Avenue
Brampton Road
Verulam School
24

Dalton St
Church St
ST PETER'S STREET
Hall Gdns
Hillside Rd
Lemsford Road
York Road
St Pauls
Clarence Road
Glenferrie Road
Blandford Road
Sandfield Rd
Harlesden Road
Burnham Rd
Royal

CATHERINE ST
Jubilee Centre
Univ
St Peter's Road
Manor Rd
St Albans City FC
Sports Ground
Laurel
Cavendish Rd
Fleetville Junior School
Fleetville Infant School

Civic Centre
Museum
Oaklands College
Almshouses
Clarence Park
Tennis Courts
Surgery
The Jamie Mosque
Cemetery
Fleetville
4
Superstore

Town Hall
Cinema
Loreto College
Liverpool Rd
Lattimore Rd
Marlborough Gate
B Pk Rd
Albion Rd
A1057
St Alban & St Stephen RC Junior/Mixed Sch
Campfield
W Pk

Law Ct
Crown Prosecution Service
VICTORIA ST B691
County Court
St Albans Station
Station W
Granville Rd
Cecil Rd
Camp Rd
Sphere Industrial Estate

HIGH ST
The Maltings Shop Centre
Abbey Stn
Lattimore Rd
Bedford Rd
Alma Rd
St Albans Synagogue
STANHOPE ROAD
Breakspear Av
Vanda Crs
Infant School
Park View Cl Cell
Camp Road

Hart Rd
A1081
Pageant Rd
Keyfield
Oswald
Ridgmont Rd
Flora Gv
Shirley Road
Edward
Delfield
Springfield Rd
5

Sopwell Lane
Albert Street
Paxton Rd
Old London Rd
Grosvenor
Victoria Square Business Area
Aspasia Close
Orchard
Kenton Gdns
Hordle Gdns
AL1
Park View Cl
Camp Prim School
St Albans Organ Mus

Bardwell Rd
Belmont Hl
LONDON RD
Riverside Rd
Cornwall Rd
University of Hertfordshire
Cunningham Hill
The Camp

E F 27 G H

St Peters JMI School
Sopwell Gdns
Ver Colne Va
Verulam Industrial Estate
Verulam Golf Club
Greenbanks
Cunningham Hill Avenue
Cunningham Hill J&I School
Foxcroft
Flinders Close

Marshalswick

ST ALBANS

Bernards Heath

Fleetville

The Camp

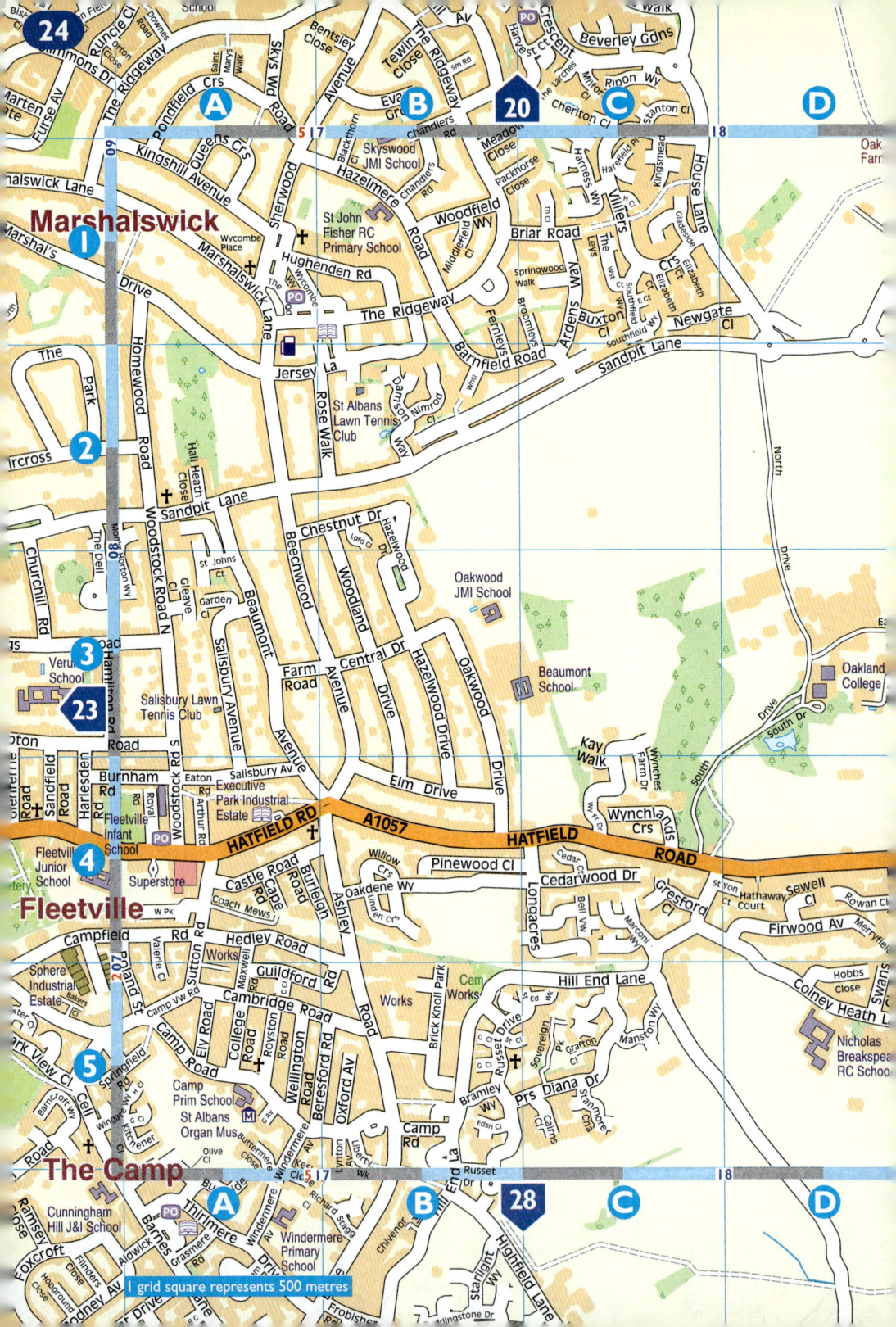

Map: Marshalswick / Fleetville / The Camp

Grid references (top)
24 | A | B | 20 | C | D

Grid references (left)
1 | 2 | 3 | 23 | 4 | 5

Grid references (bottom)
A | B | 28 | C | D

Place names
Marshalswick

Fleetville

The Camp

Streets and labels

Runcie Cl, Orton Cl, Downes, Simmons Dr, Marten Av, Furse Av, gate, The Ridgeway, Pondfield Crs, Saint Mary's Walk, Sky's Wd, Queens Crs, Road, Sherwood, Bentsley Close, Tewin Close, Eva Gr, The Ridgeway, Chandlers Rd, Blackthorn, Hazelmere Road, Skyswood JMI School, Chandlers Rd, Woodfield Wy, Middlefield Rd, Harvest Crescent, PO, Beverley Gdns, The Larches, Miller Ct, Ripon Wy, Cheriton Cl, Stanton Cl

Marshal's, Close, Kingshill Avenue, Marshalswick Lane, Wycombe Place, St John Fisher RC Primary School, Hughenden Rd, Woodfield Road, Briar Road, Harness Wy, Springwood Walk, Packhorse Close, The Leys, Villiers, Crs, Gladstone, Elizabeth Ct, House Lane, Newgate Cl, Southfield, Buxton Cl, Ardens Way, Broomleys Rd, Barnfield Road, Sandpit Lane

Drive, Homewood Road, Park, The Hall Heath Close, Jersey La, Rose Walk, St Albans Lawn Tennis Club, Damson, Nimrod Cl, Fernleys Cl

Fircross, Woodstock Road N, Sandpit Lane, Chestnut Dr, Lord Cl, Hazelwood, Woodland, Oakwood JMI School, Beaumont School, North Drive, Oakland College, South Dr, South Dr, Drive

Churchill Rd, The Dell, St Johns Ct, Cleave, Garden Ct, Beechwood, Woodland, Central Dr, Hazelwood Drive, Oakwood Drive, Kay Walk, Wynches Farm Dr, Wynchlands Crs

Verulam School, 23, Hamilton Rd, Salisbury Lawn Tennis Club, Salisbury Avenue, Beaumont Road, Farm Road, Elm Drive

Burnham Rd, Sandfield Rd, Harlesden Rd, Fleetville Infant School, Eaton Rd, Royal Rd, Arthur Rd, Woodstock Rd S, Executive Park Industrial Estate, Salisbury Av, Willow Crs, Pinewood Cl, Cedarwood Dr, Cedar Cl, Cresford Rd, Hathaway Court, Sewell Cl, Rowan Cl, Longacres, Bell Vw, St Lyon Ct, Firwood Av, Merryfield

Fleetville Junior School, Superstore, Castle Road, Cape Rd, Burleigh Rd, Ashley, Oakdene Wy, Linden Crs, HATFIELD RD, A1057, HATFIELD ROAD, Hobbs Close, Colney Heath La, Swans

Campfield Rd, Hedley Road, Works, Coach Mews, Sphere Industrial Estate, Bakers, Valerie Cl, Camp Vw Rd, Sutton Rd, Maxwell Rd, Guildford Rd, Works, Brick Knoll Park, Cem Works, Hill End Lane, Nicholas Breakspear RC School

Park View Cl, Springfield Rd, Ely Rd, College Road, Cambridge Road, Royston Rd, Wellington Rd, Beresford Rd, Oxford Av, St Ed, Sovereign Cl, Pk Grafton, Manston Wy, Colney Heath La

Cell Barn, Barncroft Wy, Kitchener, Camp Prim School, St Albans Organ Mus, Windermere Av, Keel Cl, Liberty Wk, Camp Rd, Bramley Wy, Russet Drive, Prs Diana Dr, Stanmore Cl, Cairns Cl, Edsn La

Foxcroft, Ramsey Close, Rodney Av, Hopground Close, Cunningham Hill J&I School, PO, Thirlmere, Barnes Rd, Aldwick, Grasmere Rd, Richard Stagg Cl, Windermere Primary School, Chivenor, Hill End La, Russet Dr, Highfield Lane, Starlight Wy, Frobisher Rd

28

Scale
1 grid square represents 500 metres

E Coopers Green Lane

Beech Farm
Beech Farm

F

21

G

H

19

20

60

I Cunningham Avenue

Ellenbrook

2

Oaklands Lane

A1057

St Albans Road West

Poplar Av

Poplars Close

Bramble Road

080

Bramble Road

Popefield Farm

HATFIELD ROAD

Oaklands Lane

Garden Centre

De Havilland Cl

Wilkin's

3

Green

Sm Tra

Wilkin's Green Lane

Smallford

Spring field Rd

A1057

Oaklands Lane

PO

HATFIELD ROAD

Acrewood Way

Lyon Way

4

207

Industrial Estate

The Chd

Sleapshyde

Lane

Smallford Lane

Sleapshyde Lane

Smallford Farm

Police Station

Sleapcross Gardens

A414

5

Colney Heath L

19

20

E

F

29

G

H

A414

Smallford Farm

St Marks Ch

High St

Wistlea Crs

Colney Heath JMI School

Colney

St Stephens

Park

Golf Course

Sports Arena

Abbey View

4f Club

Leisure Centre & Pool

A4147

ROAD

Hemel Hempstead Rd

Bedmond Lane

Parklands Dr

Mayne Av

Prae Wood Prim Sch

The Ran

Harry

Kingsgate

Cardinal Gv

Lane

Augustus Pl

Claudian

Lindum Pl

Flavian Cl

Deva Close

Dubrae Close

Westfields

Rowlatt Dr

Mayne Av

Meautys

Jerome Dr

Corder Cl

Westfields

Abbey

St Stephen's Avenue

Midway

Laurels Cl

Netherway

Crossfields

Midway

Allandale

Falstaff Gdns

Vicarage Cl

Marlborough School

WATFORD ROAD

ST STEPHEN'S HL

WATLING STREET

A5183

Praetorian

Vesta

Wilshere

Robert Avenue

Gillian Av

Warren Road

Butt Fld

Barn Cl

Tithe

M10

Westfields Farm

Ragged Hall Lane

Surgery

Junction 1

Hollybush Av

Cherry Hl

Corby Cl

Cuckmans Drive

Stanley

The Croft

Watford Rd

B4630

West Avenue

North Cl

South Cl

Killigrew Primary School

Greenwood Park Leisure Centre

NORTH ORBITAL ROAD

A405

Chiswell Green

Chiswell Green Lane

Chiswell Green Lane

Woodlea

Laburnum Grove

Tippendell

Barry Close

Hammers Ga

Horsemans Dr

Tippendell Lane

Carlsbrook Rd

Compton Gdns

Sunnydell

Tippendell

Orchard

Dell Rise

Drive

Park Stree

Bone Hill

Gardens of the Rose (Royal National Rose)

PO

Farmstead

B4630

Forge End

Long Fallow

Belvedere Gdns

Thistle Hotel

WATFOR

Manor

Penman Cl

N-Orbital-Rd

Wil

A405

Tennyson Rd

Driftwood Avenue

Watford Rd

Fore

NORTH ORBITAL ROAD

Maltower

Yewtree

Woodlands

Penn R

Grovelan

Walnut

Spruce

How Woo

Noke Farm

Business

1 grid square represents 500 metres

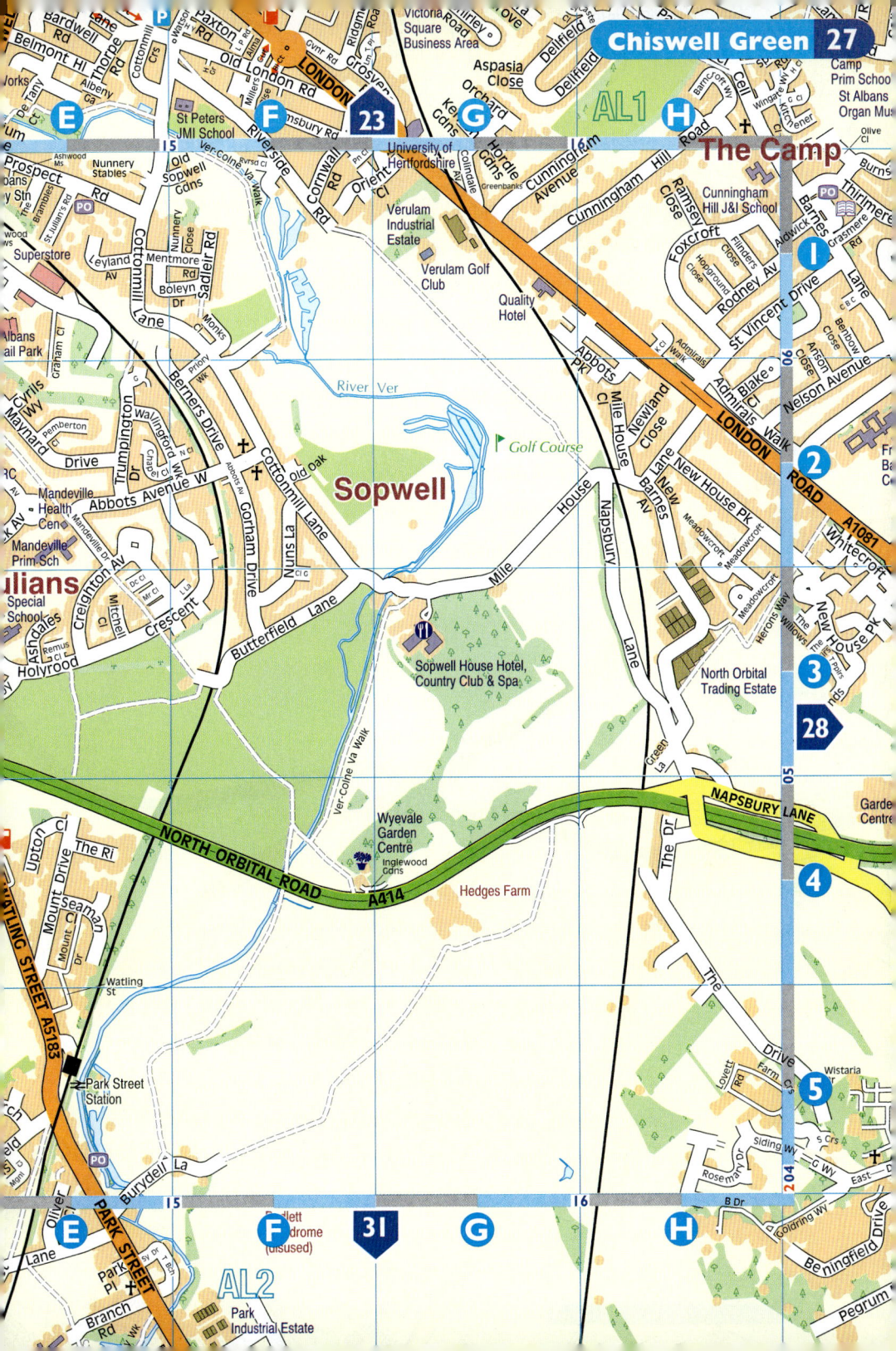

AL1

Camp
Prim Schoo
St Albans
Organ Mus

The Camp

Victoria Square Business Area
Shirley ... Gve
Delfield
Delfield
Aspasia Close
Orchard
Kel... Gdns
Hordle Gdns
Greenbanks

Bardwell Lane
Belmont Hl
Thorpe Rd
Yorks
De Tany
Albany Ga
Cottonmill Crs
Watson ...
Paxton Rd
Old London Rd
L P... Rd
Alma ...
Miller... Rd
Gvnr Rd
Grosven...
Ridg... Rd

P

E   F   23   G   H

St Peters JMI School
Riverside
Fishpond... Rd
Cornwall Rd
Orient ...
Colindale Av
University of Hertfordshire
Cunningham Hill
St Albans Rd
Cunningham Avenue
Cunningham Hill J&I School
Ramsey Close
Foxcroft
Aidwick
Barnes
Thirlmere
Crasmere
Burns

Ashwood Ms
Nunnery Stables
Prospect Rd
bans
y Stn
Brambles
St Julian's Rd
Superstore
Leyland Av
Mentmore Rd
Nunnery Close
Boleyn Dr
Sadleir Rd
Monks
Old Sopwell Gdns
Ver-Colne Va Walk

Verulam Industrial Estate
Verulam Golf Club
Quality Hotel
Abbots Pk
Abbots Cl
Mile House
Newland Close
New House Pk
Rodney Av
Flinder
Hoground
Close
Blake
BJ Cl
Anson Close
Benbow
Nelson Avenue
PO

I

Albans
ail Park
Cottonmill Lane
Graham Rd
Cyrus Wy
Maynard
Pemberton
Trumpington
Wallingford Av
Chapel
Drive
Berners Drive
Priory Wk
Old Oak
Abbots Av
Cottonmill Lane
River Ver
Sopwell
Golf Course
House Lane
Napsbury
Barnes Av
New House Pk
Meadowcroft
Herons Way
St Vincent Drive
LONDON ROAD
A1081
Whitecroft
2

Mandeville Health Cen
Mandeville Prim Sch
Creighton Av
Mitchell
DC Cl
Mr Cl
Cl G
Gorham Drive
Butterfield Lane
Mile House Lane
North Orbital Trading Estate
Meadowcroft
The Willows
New House Pk
3

ulians
Special School
Ashdales
Remus Cl
Holyrood
Crescent
Sopwell House Hotel, Country Club & Spa
Green La
The D
28

NORTH ORBITAL ROAD
Ver-Colne Va Walk
Wyevale Garden Centre
Inglewood Gdns
Hedges Farm
NAPSBURY LANE
The Dr
Garde
Centre
4

Upton Cl
The Ri
Mount Drive
Seaman
Mount
Dr
A414
The Drive
Lovett Rd
Farm Cr
Wistaria
5

WATLING STREET A5183
Watling St
Park Street Station
Rosemary Dr
Siding Wy
S Crs
East
PO

E   F   31   G   H

AL2
Park
Pl
Hadlett drome (disused)
Park Industrial Estate
Burydell La
Oliver
Lane
PARK STREET
Branch Rd
Be ingfield Drive
Goldring Wy
B Dr
Pegrum

The Camp

Camp Road
Ely R
Colle Road
Royst
Wellington Road
Beresford Rd
Oxford Av
Bric
Russell
Sovereig
Pk
Grafton
Manso
Nicholas Breakspear RC Scho

Camp Prim School
St Albans Orga
Bramley Wy
Edsn C
Prs Diana Dr
Cairns
Sn-More Cha

Springfield Rd
Barcroft Wy
Wingate W
Kitchener
Olive Cl
Buttermere Way
Windermere
Selwick Close
Richard Stagg
Lynton
Alberta Wk
A
B
24
C
D
5 17
18

Cunningham Hill J&I School
Ramsey Close
Foxcroft
Park Road
Burnside
Thirlmere
Aldwick La
Grasmere Rd
Catham Way
Windermere Primary School
Chivenor
Starlight Wy
Highfield Lane
1

St Vincent Drive
Rodney Av
Blake Cl
Arson Close
Benbow Close
Ennerdale Close
Drive
Howard Rd
Frobisher Rd
Puddingstone Dr
Ivory Cl
Bryn Wy
Church Cft
Honeycroft Dr
Tyttenhanger Green
Tyttenha

Admirals Walk
New House Pk
Meadowcroft
Nelson Avenue
Drakes
Swallow La
Crosby Close
Hill End Lane
Nightingale La
Housefield
Pitt Dr
Highfield Park Drive
Highfield Hall
Highfield Lane
2
LONDON ROAD
A1081
Whitecroft
Francis Bacon Maths & Computing College

Herons Way
The Willows
New House Pk
Cemetery
Nightingale Lane

North Trading Estate
3
27
The Almonds
Birklands La
London Road
A1081 LONDON ROAD
Nightingale La
A414

NAPSBURY LANE
Garden Centre
A414
A1081
Five Acres
4

Old Verulamiums RFC
Suffolk
Alexander
High Street
Oldfield Road
Five Acres School
Napier Wy
Perham
School
White Horse La
Horse
Lane

SHENLEY LANE B5378
The Drive
Lovett Close
Farm Crs
Wistaria Dr
Norris Cl
Lime Tree
Aubrey Av
Peters Av
Coombes Road
Harvey Rd
King's Road
Bichrs Cl
Cozenswick Cl
Cottandswick
Surgery
Wellington Road
Hertfordshire Business Cen
Morris Way
Chantry Wy
5

Rosemary Wy
Siding Wy
Goldring Wy
East Dr
Boyes Crs
Manor Road
Telford Road
Summerfield Cl
Caledon
Cherry Tree Av
Floral Dr
Obns cn
Haseldine Rd
White
Seaton Rd
High Street
Meadow
Sanders Close
Willowby Av
Kennedy
LONDON COLNEY

B Dr
Beningfield
Drive
Azalea Close
A
B
32
C
Coliyer Rd
Bluebe
PO
Riverside
Walsingham
Fieldfares
Burr C
Barn
5 17
18

1 grid square represents 500 metres

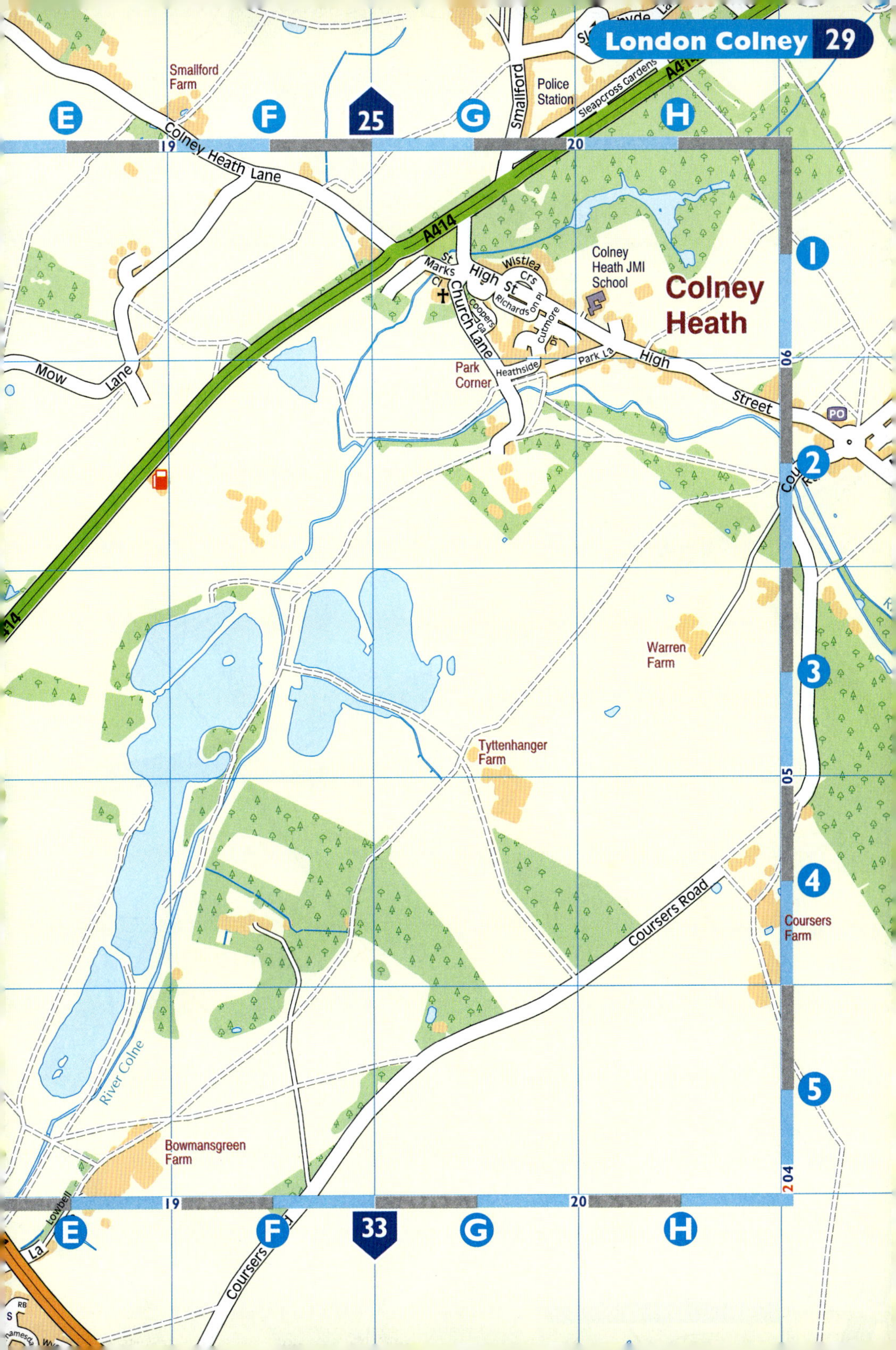

E F **25** G H

Smallford
Farm

Colney Heath Lane

Smallford

Police
Station

Sleapcross Gardens

A414

I

St.
Marks

High
St

Wistlea
Crs

Colney
Heath JMI
School

Richards Cl. Pl

Coopers Cl

Cuthmore
Dr

**Colney
Heath**

Church Lane

Park
Corner

Heathside

Park La.

High

Street

2

Mow

Lane

PO

Warren
Farm

3

Tyttenhanger
Farm

Coursers Road

4

Coursers
Farm

River Colne

5

Bowmansgreen
Farm

E F **33** G H

Coursers
La

RB
S

A   **B**   **26**   **C**   **D**

5 13   14

Compton Gdns
Farnham
B4630
Tippendell Lane
Sunnydell
Tennison Rd
Park
Stre

Long Fallow
Forge End
WATFORD ROAD
Manor Rd
Willow Way
Redring Dr
Dell Rise
Drive

Belvedere Gdns
NORTH ORBITAL ROAD
Mayflower Road
Penn Road
Tipp

Noke Farm
Thistle Hotel
Penman Cl
Forefield
N-Orbital-Rd
A405
Woodlands
Pilgrin
Pilgrim
Close

Business Centre
NORTH ORBITAL ROAD
Spruce
Walnut Cl
Yewtree
Grovelands
How Wood
Fairway Close
Ring Way Rd
PO
How Woo

1
Noke Lane
Spooners
The Mall
Burston Dr

2
Junction 21a
Lye Lane
Tenterden House
Bay tree Cl
Alder Cl
Birchwood Wy
How Wood
Whitebeams End
Withy Wd
Park St Lane
Slowmans

Applecroft
Elms
Wych
St Albans Musical Museum
M
J Davies
Hertford End

NORTH ORBITAL ROAD
03
M25
Lye Lane
Hazel Road
Homewood Independent School
Harbert Gdns
Maplefield Acers
Maplefield
Maplefield
Black Wd Cl
Park Street Lane

3
Watford Road
Ryall Cl
Field Cl
Reynard's Wy
Oakwood
Oakridge
Five Acres Av
Stratford Wy
Garnett Dri
The Meads
Reedham
Smug Oak Green Business Cen
Horseshoe Business Park

Short Lane
Woodside Rd
Silver Trees
Riding

4
Broad Acre
Jenkins Avenue
Jordan's Way
Ashridge
Hornbeams
Wildwood Av
Pine Gv
Moss Side
Brackendene
Drive
PO
Hamlet Cl
West
N Riding
South Riding
Oak Av
Lye Lane
Black Boy Wd
Smug Oak Lane
Smug Oak
Works
Bricket Wood Station
Bricket Wood Sports Centre

Larch Av
Mab Close
Rosedale
Bluebird
Mount
Pleasant
Randalls
Halifax Cl
Yule Cl
St Lawrence Wy
Mt Pleasant La
The Crs
Hamilton Cl
Rowan Cl
Hunters Ride
Claremont
Station Rd
Drop Lane
Training Centre

5
The Kestrels
Bucknalls
Bucknalls Dr
Enid Cl
Moran Cl
Hampstead Cl
Ferndene Cl
Ash Copse Cl
Bricket Wood
Bricket Wood Common
Valley Walk

Pleasant Lane School

5 13   14

A   **B**   **C**   **D**

Lane

1 grid square represents 500 metres

Park Street
Station

E
PO

F

27

G

H

Siding Wy
S Crs
G Wy
East Dr

Rosemary Dr

Burydell La

15

16

04

Coldring Wy

Beningfield Drive

Oliver
Park St

Park Street
PI

Branch
Rd

PARK STREET

Valley Vw

Ver-Colne Valley Wk

Lane

B Dr

I

Pegrum D

Radlett
Aerodrome
(disused)

AL2

Park
Industrial Estate

Stroud Wood
Business Centre

Curo Park

Brinsmead

FROGMORE

Park Street CE
mary School

Watermeadow

Lane

Minster Ct

Hyde La

Frogmore

2

03

A5183

Hampden
Place

RADLETT

Moor MI La

Ventura Park

3

32

M25

Premier
Travel
Inn

Moor MI

Smug Oak La

**Colney
Street**

ROAD

Old Parkbury La

Handley
Page Wy

Old
Parkbury

4

P

Works

02

River Ver

E

15

F

16

G

Harper Lane

56

5

HARPER LANE

H

p Lane

River Colne

Netherwyde
Farm

A

Houndswood

LONDON
COLNEY

A B 28 C D

I

2

3

31

4

5

A B C D

Drive
Wistaria
Dr
Farm Crs
Norris Cl
S Crs
G Wy
Siding Wy
East
Boyes
Goldring Wy
Lime Tree Wy
B5378
Cott
Road
Harvey Rd
Napsbury Av
King's Road
Surgery
Manor Road
Summerfield
Caledon
Cherry Tree Av
Floral
Dr
Cons on
Chantry La
High Street
Jubilee
Kennedy
White
Horse
Seaton
Rd
Willowby
Sanders
Close
Meadow
Road
Close
PO
Richardson
Cl
Burr Cl
Riverside
Industrial
Estate
Barr
Rosemary Dr
B Dr
Goldring Wy
Beningfield Drive
Azalea
Close
Pegrum Drive
Shenley
Lane
Bedford
Road
Colliver Rd
Walsingham
Wy
Primary
School
St Annes Road
Fieldfares
Hardwicke
Broadoake Cl
Bluers
Rd
Lakeside Place
Reed
Waterside
Waterside
Willowside
River Colne
Shenley Lane
SHENLEY LANE
Nature
Reserve
Broad
Colney
Superstore
03
04
02
M25
BELL
B5378
Pastoral
Centre
31
HARPER LANE
B556
Forest Lane
Heath Lime
Way
Meadow Av
Meadow Cl
Ridgeway
Haperbury
Hospital
Shenleybury
Clore
Shalom
Sch
Farm Cl
SHENLEYBURY
Shenleybury
Cottages
HARPER LANE
B556
The Common
Radlett
Lodge
School
Queens Way
Bell
North Av
Headingley
Close
Edgbaston Drive
Trent Gr
Wild

1 grid square represents 500 metres

E
Bowmansgreen Farm F 29 G H

River Co

Lowbell Lane

La

Wyedale

RB

Coursers Road

Eskdale THE BELL ROUNDABOUT

Ridgeview

Br Rd

Ridgeview

A1081 Junction 22

ey Fields
pping

M25

A1081 B556

B556

I

2

04

03

Salisbury Hall

M De Havilland Aircraft
Heritage Centre &
Mosquito Aircraft Museum

Redwell Wood
Farm

3

B556

Shenley
Lodge

Manor
Lodge
School

Ridgehill

M25

4

BLACKHO

Rectory Lane

2 02

Southridge

5

Packhorse

E F G H

Combe
Wood

Rectory Lane

Lane

Rabley
Farm

Amwell 14 B2	Coleman Green................15 F4	How Wood 30 D1	St Albans........................2
Ayres End 13 G4	Colney Street..................31 F4	Kinsbourne Green.............5 E1	St Julians........................26
Batford 7 F3	Cooper's Green 21 G4	Leasey Bridge 7 G5	St Stephens.....................26
Bernards Heath 3 F1	Cromer-Hyde 15 H4	Lea Valley 7 G3	Sandridge.......................20
Bricket Wood...............30 A5	Ellenbrook....................25 H1	London Colney 28 D5	Shenleybury....................32
Broad Colney 32 C2	Fleetville 23 H4	Mackerye End.................7 F2	Sleapshyde.....................25
The Camp 27 H1	The Folly 8 A4	Marshalls Heath 7 H3	Smallford........................25
Childwick Bury 18 D3	Friar's Wash..................4 A3	Marshalswick 23 H1	Smug Oak.......................30
Childwick Green 18 C2	Frogmore 31 F2	New Greens 18 D4	Sopwell..........................27
Chiswell Green.............26 A4	Gustard Wood 8 B2	Nomansland....................14 B3	Townsend........................2
Church End 10 D5	Harpenden 6 A5	Park Street....................26 D5	Tyttenhanger...................28
Cold Harbour 6 D1	Harpenden Common 12 C2	Redbourn 11 E3	Waterend.......................15
Coleman Green............15 F4	Hatching Green 12 A3	Redbournbury.................17 H2	Wheathampstead..............8

USING THE STREET INDEX

Street names are listed alphabetically. Each street name is followed by its postal town or area locality, the Postcode District, the page number, and the reference to the square in which the name is found.

Standard index entries are shown as follows:

Abbey Av *STALW/RED* AL3..............**26** B2

Street names and selected addresses not shown on the map due to scale restrictions are shown in the index with an asterisk:

Abbey Ms *STAL* AL1 * **2** C7

GENERAL ABBREVIATIONS

ACC ....ACCESS	E ....EAST	LDG ....LODGE	R ....RIV
ALY ....ALLEY	EMB ....EMBANKMENT	LGT ....LIGHT	RBT ....ROUNDABO
AP...............APPROACH	EMBY ....EMBASSY	LK....................LOCK	RD...................RO
AR................ARCADE	ESP ....ESPLANADE	LKS.................LAKES	RDG................RI
ASS...........ASSOCIATION	EST ....ESTATE	LNDG ....LANDING	REP.............REPUE
AV................AVENUE	EX ....EXCHANGE	LTL ....LITTLE	RES.............RESERV
BCH ....BEACH	EXPY ....EXPRESSWAY	LWR ....LOWER	RFC....RUGBY FOOTBALL C
BLDS ....BUILDINGS	EXT ....EXTENSION	MAG ....MAGISTRATE	RI....................F
BND................BEND	F/O ....FLYOVER	MAN ....MANSIONS	RP...................RA
BNK.................BANK	FC ....FOOTBALL CLUB	MD ....MEAD	RW...................R
BR..................BRIDGE	FK....................FORK	MDW ....MEADOWS	S....................SO
BRK................BROOK	FLD ....FIELD	MEM ....MEMORIAL	SCH................SCH
BTM..............BOTTOM	FLDS ....FIELDS	MI....................MILL	SE ....SOUTH E
BUS..............BUSINESS	FLS ....FALLS	MKT ....MARKET	SER...........SERVICE A
BVD ....BOULEVARD	FM ....FARM	MKTS ....MARKETS	SH...................SH
BY.................BYPASS	FT ....FORT	ML ....MALL	SHOP.............SHOPP
CATH ....CATHEDRAL	FTS ....FLATS	MNR ....MANOR	SKWY.............SKW
CEM ....CEMETERY	FWY ....FREEWAY	MS ....MEWS	SMT ....SUM
CEN ....CENTRE	FY ....FERRY	MSN ....MISSION	SOC................SOCI
CFT ....CROFT	GA..................GATE	MT ....MOUNT	SP ....S
CH ....CHURCH	GAL ....GALLERY	MTN ....MOUNTAIN	SPR................SPR
CHA ....CHASE	GDN ....GARDEN	MTS ....MOUNTAINS	SQ ....SQU
CHYD ....CHURCHYARD	GDNS ....GARDENS	MUS ....MUSEUM	ST....................STR
CIR ....CIRCLE	GLD ....GLADE	MWY ....MOTORWAY	STN ....STAT
CIRC ....CIRCUS	GLN ....GLEN	N ....NORTH	STR ....STRE
CL...................CLOSE	GN ....GREEN	NE.............NORTH EAST	STRD..............STRA
CLFS ....CLIFFS	GRA ....GROUND	NW...........NORTH WEST	SW ....SOUTH W
CMP ....CAMP	GRA ....GRANGE	O/P ....OVERPASS	TDG ....TRAD
CNR ....CORNER	GRG ....GARAGE	OFF ....OFFICE	TER..............TERRA
CO..................COUNTY	GT ....GREAT	ORCH ....ORCHARD	THWY ....THROUGHW
COLL ....COLLEGE	GTWY ....GATEWAY	OV....................OVAL	TNL ....TUN
COM ....COMMON	GV..................GROVE	PAL ....PALACE	TOLL ....TOLL
COMM ....COMMISSION	HGR ....HIGHER	PAS ....PASSAGE	TPK ....TURNF
CON ....CONVENT	HL ....HILL	PAV ....PAVILION	TR ....TRA
COT ....COTTAGE	HLS ....HILLS	PDE ....PARADE	TRL ....TR
COTS ....COTTAGES	HO ....HOUSE	PH ....PUBLIC HOUSE	TWR ....TOV
CP...................CAPE	HOL ....HOLLOW	PK...................PARK	U/P ....UNDERP
CPS ....COPSE	HOSP ....HOSPITAL	PKWY ....PARKWAY	UNI ....UNIVERS
CR...................CREEK	HRB ....HARBOUR	PL ....PLACE	UPR ....UPF
CREM ....CREMATORIUM	HTH ....HEATH	PLN ....PLAIN	V......................V
CRS ....CRESCENT	HTS ....HEIGHTS	PLNS ....PLAINS	VA.................VAL
CSWY ....CAUSEWAY	HVN ....HAVEN	PLZ ....PLAZA	VIAD..............VIADU
CT..................COURT	HWY ....HIGHWAY	POL ....POLICE STATION	VIL VI
CTRL ....CENTRAL	IMP ....IMPERIAL	PR ....PRINCE	VIS VI
CTS ....COURTS	IN....................INLET	PREC ....PRECINCT	VLG ....VILL/
CTYD ....COURTYARD	IND EST....INDUSTRIAL ESTATE	PREP ....PREPARATORY	VLS VIL
CUTT ....CUTTINGS	INF ....INFIRMARY	PRIM ....PRIMARY	VW V
CV...................COVE	INFO ....INFORMATION	PROM ....PROMENADE	W ....W
CYN ....CANYON	INT ....INTERCHANGE	PRS ....PRINCESS	WD................WC
DEPT ....DEPARTMENT	IS..................ISLAND	PRT ....PORT	WHF ....WH/
DL...................DALE	JCT ....JUNCTION	PT ....POINT	WK..................WA
DM ....DAM	JTY ....JETTY	PTH ....PATH	WKS ....WA
DR...................DRIVE	KG ....KING	PZ ....PIAZZA	WLS ....WE
DRO ....DROVE	KNL ....KNOLL	QD ....QUADRANT	WY V
DRY ....DRIVEWAY	L.....................LAKE	QU ....QUEEN	YD...................YA
DWGS ....DWELLINGS	LA ....LANE	QY ....QUAY	YHA ....YOUTH HOS

POSTCODE TOWNS AND AREA ABBREVIATIONS

HARP.................Harpenden	LCOL/BKTW ....London Colney/	STALE/WH.............St Albans east/	WLYN................Welw
HAT...................Hatfield	...................Bricket Wood	..............Wheathampstead	
HHNE ....Hemel Hempstead	RAD.....................Radlett	STALW/RED ....St Albans west/	
...................northeast	STAL...................St Albans	..................Redbourn	

A

ey Av STALW/RED AL3 ....26 B2
ey Ms STAL AL1 * 2 C7
ey Mill End STALW/RED AL3 .....2 A7
ey Mill La STALW/RED AL3 ....2 A7
ey View Rd STALW/RED AL3 ......2 A5
ot John Ms STALE/WH AL4........8 C5
ots Av STAL AL1 ....27 F2
ots Av West STAL AL1 ....27 F2
ots Pk STAL AL1 ....27 G2
cia Wk HARP AL5 ....13 E3
rs LCOL/BKTW AL2 ....30 D2
Acorns STALE/WH AL4 * 24 C4
ewood Wy STALE/WH AL4 ....25 E4
laide St STALW/RED AL3 ....2 D4
mirals Wk HARP AL5 ....27 H2
man Cl STALW/RED AL3 * 26 A1
an Av STALW/RED AL3 ....2 C2
an Pk STALW/RED AL4 ....25 E4
any Ms LCOL/BKTW AL2 * 30 B1
eny Ga STAL AL1 ....23 E5
ert St STAL AL1 ....2 C7
ion Rd STAL AL1 ....3 H6
ury Cl STALE/WH AL4 ....20 B4
er Cl LCOL/BKTW AL2 ....30 C2
ers End La HARP AL5 ....6 A4
wick STAL AL1 ....27 H1
wickbury Crs HARP AL5 ....7 E5
wick Rd HARP AL5 ....13 F1
ander Rd LCOL/BKTW AL2 .....28 B4
andra STAL AL1 ....3 F6
ndale STALW/RED AL3 ....26 C2
n Cl STALE/WH AL4 ....14 C2
a Cut STAL AL1 ....23 F5
a Rd STAL AL1 ....3 F7
Almonds STAL AL1 ....28 A3
p Cl LCOL/BKTW AL2 ....32 D2
orp Rd STAL AL1 ....3 F4
wood HARP AL5 ....7 E5
erton STALW/RED AL3 ....22 D1
ey Gdns HARP AL5 ....13 E1
perley Cl HARP AL5 ....6 C4
oleside HARP AL5 * 6 D4
orose La HARP AL5 ....6 B3
well La STALE/WH AL4 ....14 A2
ables La HARP AL5 ....4 C2
on Cl STAL AL1 ....28 A1
TALE/WH AL4 ....20 B3
onine Ga STALW/RED AL3 ......22 B5
il Pl LCOL/BKTW AL2 * 26 B5
ns Cl HARP AL5 ....6 B4
lecroft LCOL/BKTW AL2 ....30 C2
letree Gv STALW/RED AL3 ......11 E3
lewood HARP AL5 ....5 H3
roach Rd STAL AL1 ....23 F5
n Cl HARP AL5 ....13 E3
ners Flds STAL AL1 ....3 G1
en Gv HARP AL5 ....6 C5
ens Marsh STALE/WH AL4 *......24 C4
ens Wy STALE/WH AL4 ....24 C2
astrong Cl LCOL/BKTW AL2......32 D1
etine Cl STALW/RED AL3 ....26 A1
nal STAL AL1 ....24 A4
san Crs STALW/RED AL3 ....2 A3
ndel Gv STALW/RED AL3 ......19 E5
bourne Ct STALE/WH AL4......28 B1
by Gdns STAL AL1 ....27 E3
Copse LCOL/BKTW AL2 ....30 A5
croft STAL AL1 ....13 F1
dales STAL AL1 ....27 E3
Gv STALE/WH AL4 ....8 B5
ley Gdns HARP AL5 ....5 C3
ley Rd STAL AL1 ....24 B4
tree Ct STAL AL1 ....3 G6
well Pk STALE/WH AL4 ....3 E5
well St STALE/WH AL4 ....2 C3
wood Ms STAL AL1 ....27 E1
asia Cl STAL AL1 ....23 C5
prey Av LCOL/BKTW AL2 ......28 B5
prey La STALE/WH AL4 ....16 B2
ugustus Ct STALW/RED AL3 ......26 A1
n St STAL AL1 ....3 F3
nue St Nicholas HARP AL5 ......6 B5
cet Cl STALW/RED AL3 ....22 D1
es End La HARP AL5 ....13 E5
garth HARP AL5 ....12 C1
garth Rd STALW/RED AL3 ......10 D3
lea Cl LCOL/BKTW AL2 ....32 B1

B

lingham Dr HARP AL5............11 H1
ters Cl STAL AL1 ....3 K7

Balfour Ct HARP AL5 ....6 D3
Bamville Wd HARP AL5 * 12 D4
Bardwell Ct STAL AL1 ....2 C7
Bardwell Rd STAL AL1 ....2 C7
Barley Mow La STALE/WH AL4...28 D2
Barley Ri HARP AL5 * 6 D5
Barlings Rd HARP AL5 ....12 C4
Barncroft Wy STAL AL1 ....23 H5
Barnet Rd LCOL/BKTW AL2 ......32 D1
Barnfield Ct HARP AL5 ....12 D1
Barnfield Rd HARP AL5 ....12 D1
    STALE/WH AL4............24 B2
Barns Dene HARP AL5 ....5 H4
Barrons Rw HARP AL5 ....13 E2
Barry Ct LCOL/BKTW AL2 ....26 C4
Barton Cl HARP AL5 ....6 D3
Barton Rd STALE/WH AL4 ....14 B1
Bassett Ct STALW/RED AL3......11 E4
Batchwood Dr STALW/RED AL3...22 D1
Batchwood Gdns
    STALW/RED AL3 ....23 E1
Batchwood Vw STALW/RED AL3...2 C7
Batford Ml HARP AL5 * 7 E4
Batford Rd HARP AL5 ....7 E4
Battlefield Rd STAL AL1 ....3 G2
Battleview STALE/WH AL4 ....14 D1
Bay Tree Cl LCOL/BKTW AL2 ......30 C1
Beaconsfield Rd STAL AL1 ....3 H6
Beaumonds STAL AL1 * 2 E5
Beaumont Av STAL AL1 ....24 A3
Beaumont Hall La
    STALW/RED AL3 ....17 F2
Beckett's Av STALW/RED AL3 ......22 D1
Bedford Park Rd STAL AL1 ....3 F6
Bedford Rd STAL AL1 ....3 F7
Bedmond La STALW/RED AL3......26 A1
Beech Bottom STALW/RED AL3...23 E1
Beech Crs HARP AL5 ....12 D4
Beech Crs STALE/WH AL4 ....14 C2
The Beeches LCOL/BKTW AL2......31 E1
Beech Farm Dr STALE/WH AL4......21 E5
Beechfield Cl STALW/RED AL3 * ...11 E4
Beech Hyde La STALE/WH AL4......15 E2
Beeching Cl HARP AL5............6 C2
Beech Pl STALW/RED AL3 * 23 E1
Beech Rdg HARP AL5 * 6 D5
Beech Rd STALW/RED AL3 ....23 F1
Beechwood Av STAL AL1 ....24 A2
Beesonend La HARP AL5 ....18 A1
    STALW/RED AL3 ....17 G2
Belgrave Cl STALE/WH AL4 ....20 B5
Bellchambers Cl
    LCOL/BKTW AL2............28 B5
Bell La LCOL/BKTW AL2............32 D1
The Bell Rbt LCOL/BKTW AL2......33 F1
Bell Vw STALE/WH AL4 ....24 C1
Belmont Hl STAL AL1 ....2 C7
Belsize Ct STALE/WH AL4 ....20 B4
Belvedere Gdns
    STALW/RED AL3 ....30 A1
Ben Austins STALW/RED AL3......10 D5
Benbow Cl STAL AL1 ....28 A1
Beningfield Dr LCOL/BKTW AL2......31 H1
Bentley Ct STALE/WH AL4 ....20 C5
Beresford Rd STAL AL1 ....24 B5
Berkley Ct STALE/WH AL4 ....20 B5
Bernard St STALW/RED AL3......2 D4
ur Rd STAL AL1 ....3 H5
Berners Dr STAL AL1 ....27 E2
The Berries STALW/RED AL3......19 H5
Betjeman Cl HARP AL5 * 6 D5
Bettespol Mdw STALW/RED AL3...10 D3
Beverley Gdns STALW/RED AL3...20 C3
Bewdley Ct HARP AL5 ....13 E3
Birchmead Cl STALW/RED AL3 * ...23 E1
Birch Wy HARP AL5 ....12 C1
    LCOL/BKTW AL2............32 C1
Birchwood Wy LCOL/BKTW AL2...30 C2
Birklands La STAL AL1 ....24 B3
Birklands Pk STAL AL1 * 28 A3
Bishop's Cl STALE/WH AL4 ....19 H5
Black Boy Wd LCOL/BKTW AL2...30 B4
Black Cut STAL AL1 ....23 F5
Black Green Wood Cl
    LCOL/BKTW AL2............30 C3
Blackhorse La STALW/RED AL3...10 D3
Blacksmith's La STALW/RED AL3...22 C4
Blackthorn La STAL AL1 ....24 B1
Blake Cl STAL AL1 ....27 H2
Blandford Rd STAL AL1 ....3 J5
Blenheim Rd STAL AL1 ....3 H5
Blenkin Cl STALW/RED AL3......18 D5
Bloomfield Rd HARP AL5 ....6 A1
Blueberry Cl STALE/WH AL4......19 E5
Bluebird Wy LCOL/BKTW AL2......30 A4
Bluehouse Hl STALE/WH AL4......22 D5
Bluett Rd LCOL/BKTW AL2 ....32 C1
Blundell Cl STALW/RED AL3......19 E5
Boissy Cl STALE/WH AL4 ....24 D5
Boleyn Dr STAL AL1 ....27 F1

Bolingbrook STALE/WH AL4......19 H5
Boundary Rd STAL AL1 ....3 F2
The Bourne HARP AL5 ....6 A4
Bower Heath La HARP AL5......6 D1
Bower's Pde HARP AL5 ....6 D5
Bowers Wy HARP AL5 ....6 B4
Bowes Lyon Ms STALW/RED AL3...2 C6
Bowgate STAL AL1 ....3 F3
Bowling Cl HARP AL5 ....6 A1
Boyes Crs LCOL/BKTW AL2......28 A5
Brache Cl STALW/RED AL3......10 D4
Brackendale Gv HARP AL5.........5 G3
Brackenden LCOL/BKTW AL2......30 A4
Bramble Cl HARP AL5 ....6 A3
Bramble Rd HAT AL10 ....25 H3
The Brambles STAL AL1 ....27 E1
Bramley Wy STALE/WH AL4......24 B5
Brampton Cl HARP AL5 ....7 E5
Brampton Rd STAL AL1 ....3 J4
Branch Rd LCOL/BKTW AL2......31 E1
    STALW/RED AL3 ....22 C3
Breadcroft La HARP AL5 ....6 C4
Breakspear Av STAL AL1 ....3 H7
Brecken Cl STALE/WH AL4......19 H5
Brewhouse Hl STALE/WH AL4......14 B1
Briar Rd STAL AL1 ....24 B1
Bricket Rd STAL AL1 ....2 D5
Brick Knoll Pk STAL AL1 ....24 B5
Bride Hall La WLYN AL6 ....9 F2
Bridle Cl STALW/RED AL3 ....3 F1
Brinklow Ct STALW/RED AL3......26 C2
Brinsmead LCOL/BKTW AL2......31 E1
Britton Av STALW/RED AL3 ....2 C5
Broadfields HARP AL5 ....6 A4
Broadlake Cl LCOL/BKTW AL2......32 C1
Broadstone Rd HARP AL5 ....12 D3
The Broadway STAL AL1 * 2 D5
    STALE/WH AL4............8 A1
Brocket Vw STALE/WH AL4 ....14 C1
Brooke End STALW/RED AL3......10 D5
Brooklands Ct STAL AL1 * 2 E5
Broom Cnr HARP AL5 * 12 D1
Broomfield LCOL/BKTW AL2......30 D1
Broomleys STAL AL1 ....24 B1
Browning Rd HARP AL5 ....6 A4
Bryant Ct HARP AL5 ....6 B3
Bryn Wy STALW/RED AL3......28 C1
Bucknalls Dr LCOL/BKTW AL2......30 A5
Bull La STALW/RED AL3 ....14 H3
Bull Rd HARP AL5 ....12 C1
The Bungalows HARP AL5 ....6 D3
Burleigh Rd STAL AL1 ....24 A4
Burnham Rd STAL AL1 ....3 K5
Burnsall Pl HARP AL5 ....12 D3
Burnside STAL AL1 ....28 A1
Burr Cl LCOL/BKTW AL2 ....30 D2
Burston Dr LCOL/BKTW AL2......30 D2
Burton Cl STALE/WH AL4 ....8 B1
Burydell La LCOL/BKTW AL2......31 E1
Bury Gn STALW/RED AL3 ....14 B1
Burywick HARP AL5 ....12 C4
Butterfield La STAL AL1 ....27 F3
Butterfield Rd STALE/WH AL4......14 B2
Buttermere Cl STAL AL1 ....24 A5
Butt Field Vw STAL AL1 ....26 D3
Buxton Cl STALE/WH AL4 ....24 D5
Byron Rd HARP AL5 ....6 B4

C

Caesars Rd STALE/WH AL4 ....14 C1
Cairns Cl STALE/WH AL4 ....24 C5
Calbury Ct STAL AL1 ....24 A5
Caledon Rd LCOL/BKTW AL2......28 B5
Camberley Pl HARP AL5 ....13 E3
Cambridge Rd STAL AL1 ....24 A5
Camfield Rd STAL AL1 ....3 K6
Camp Rd STAL AL1 ....3 H6
Camp View Rd STAL AL1 ....24 A5
Canberra Cl STALW/RED AL3......19 G5
Cannon St STALW/RED AL3 ....2 C4
Canons Fld STALE/WH AL4 ....8 C5
Cape Rd STAL AL1 ....24 A4
Cardinal Gv STALW/RED AL3......26 C1
Carisbrooke Rd HARP AL5 ....6 D4
Carisbrook Rd LCOL/BKTW AL2...26 C5
Carlisle Av STALW/RED AL3 ....2 D2
Carlton Bank HARP AL5 * 6 C5
Carlton Rd HARP AL5 ....6 C5
Carnegie Rd STALW/RED AL3......19 E5
Carpenders Cl HARP AL5 ....5 G2
Carters Yd STAL AL1 * 2 C5
Castle Ri STALE/WH AL4 ....7 G4
Castle Rd STAL AL1 ....3 G5
Catham Cl STAL AL1 ....28 A1
Catherine St STALW/RED AL3......2 D4

Cavan Dr STALW/RED AL3............19 E4
Cavan Rd STALW/RED AL3............10 D3
Cavendish Rd STAL AL1 ....3 H6
Cecil Rd STAL AL1 ....3 H6
Cedar Ct STALE/WH AL4 ....24 C4
The Cedars HARP AL5 ....6 C5
Cedarwood Dr STALE/WH AL4......24 C4
Cell Barnes Cl STAL AL1 ....28 A1
Cell Barnes La STAL AL1 ....23 H5
    STAL AL1............28 A2
Central Dr STAL AL1 ....24 B3
Century Cl STALW/RED AL3............2 B3
Chalfont Pl STAL AL1 * 2 E5
Chalkdell Flds STALE/WH AL4......23 H1
Chamberlaines HARP AL5 ....4 D1
Chancery Cl STALE/WH AL4............20 C4
Chandlers Rd STALE/WH AL4......24 B1
Chantry La LCOL/BKTW AL2......28 C5
Chapel Cl STAL AL1 ....27 E2
Chapel Pl STAL AL1 * 27 E2
Charlotte Cl STALE/WH AL4......24 C4
Charmouth Ct STAL AL1 ....23 H1
Charmouth Rd STAL AL1 ....3 J2
Chene Dr STALW/RED AL3............2 C2
The Chennies HARP AL5 * 12 D2
Chequer La STALW/RED AL3............10 D5
Chequer St STAL AL1............2 C6
Cheriton Cl STALE/WH AL4............20 C5
Cherry Hl LCOL/BKTW AL2............26 B4
Cherry Tree Av LCOL/BKTW AL2...28 C5
Cherry Tree La STALE/WH AL4......7 H4
Chester Gibbons Gn
    LCOL/BKTW AL2............28 C5
Chesterton Av HARP AL5 ....6 D5
Chestnut Dr STAL AL1 ....24 A2
Chicken La LCOL/BKTW AL2 * ...32 C1
Chiltern Rd STALE/WH AL4......20 B5
Chime Sq STALW/RED AL3............2 E3
Chivenor Pl STALE/WH AL4......28 B1
The Chowns HARP AL5 ....12 B4
Christchurch Cl STALW/RED AL3...2 B5
Christopher Pl STALW/RED AL3...2 C6
Church Crs STALE/WH AL4......28 B1
Church Cft STALE/WH AL4......28 B1
Church End STALE/WH AL4......20 B2
    STALW/RED AL3............10 D5
Churchfield HARP AL5 ....12 D1
Church Gn HARP AL5 ....6 C5
Church Green Rw HARP AL5 *......6 B5
Churchill Rd STAL AL1 ....3 K3
Church La STAL AL1 ....29 C1
Church St STALE/WH AL4 ....14 C1
    STALW/RED AL3............2 D4
Church Vw STALE/WH AL4 * 14 C1
Civic Centre STAL AL1 * 2 D5
Claremont LCOL/BKTW AL2......30 B5
Clarence Rd HARP AL5 ....6 B4
    STAL AL1............3 H5
Clarendon Rd HARP AL5 ....6 C5
Claudian Pl STALW/RED AL3......26 B1
Claygate Av HARP AL5 ....5 H4
The Cleave HARP AL5 ....7 E5
Clifton St STAL AL1 ....2 C5
Cloister Garth STAL AL1 ....27 F3
Cloisters HARP AL5 * 12 D3
The Close HARP AL5 ....5 G2
    STAL AL1............26 D2
Coach Ms STAL AL1 ....24 A4
Codicote Rd STALE/WH AL4......8 D5
    STALE/WH AL4............9 E4
Coldharbour La HARP AL5......6 C2
Coleman Green La
    STALE/WH AL4............20 C1
Coleswood Rd HARP AL5......12 D2
Colindale Av STAL AL1 ....27 G1
College Pl STALW/RED AL3......2 B5
College Rd STAL AL1 ....24 A5
College St STALW/RED AL3 ....2 C5
Collens Rd HARP AL5 ....12 C4
Collingwood Dr LCOL/BKTW AL2...28 C4
Collyer Rd LCOL/BKTW AL2......32 C1
Colnbrook Cl LCOL/BKTW AL2......32 D1
Colne Gdns LCOL/BKTW AL2......32 C1
Colney Heath La STALE/WH AL4...24 C5
The Colonnade
    STALW/RED AL3 * 2 C5
Common La HARP AL5 ....7 E1
The Common HARP AL5 ....5 E2
    RAD WD7............32 A5
    STALW/RED AL3............11 E4
Compton Gdns LCOL/BKTW AL2...26 C5
Coningsby Bank STAL AL1......26 D3
Connaught Rd HARP AL5......6 C4
    STALW/RED AL3............2 B1
Conquerors Hl STALE/WH AL4......14 D1
Coombes Rd LCOL/BKTW AL2......28 B5
Coopers Ga STAL AL1 ....29 C1
Coopers Green La HAT AL10......21 H3
    STALE/WH AL4............25 E1

Coopers Meadow
  STALW/RED AL3 ....10 D3
Cooters End La *HARP* AL5...........6 A2
Copper Beeches *HARP* AL5...........6 C5
Corby Cl *LCOL/BKTW* AL2 ....26 B4
Corder Cl *STALW/RED* AL3...........26 B2
Corinium Ga *STALW/RED* AL3...........26 B1
Cornwall Rd *HARP* AL5...........6 C4
  STAL AL1...........27 F1
Corringham Ct *STAL* AL1...........3 G4
Cory-Wright Wy
  STALE/WH AL4...........8 D5
Cotlandswick *LCOL/BKTW* AL2...28 B4
Cotsmoor *STAL* AL1...........3 H6
Cotswold Cl *STALE/WH* AL4 ....20 B4
Cottonmill Crs *STAL* AL1...........23 E5
Cottonmill La *STAL* AL1...........27 E1
Coursers Rd *LCOL/BKTW* AL2...33 F1
  STALE/WH AL4...........29 H4
Courtfields *HARP* AL5...........7 E5
Courtside *STALW/RED* AL3 * 2 B2
The Courtyard *STALE/WH* AL4 ....25 E4
Cowper Rd *HARP* AL5...........6 C5
Crabtree La *HARP* AL5...........12 D1
Craiglands *STALE/WH* AL4...........20 C5
Cranbourne Dr *HARP* AL5...........12 D3
Cranbrook Dr *STALE/WH* AL4 ....24 D4
Cravells Rd *HARP* AL5...........12 D3
Crecy Gdns *STALW/RED* AL3 ....10 D3
Creighton Av *STAL* AL1...........27 E3
The Crescent *LCOL/BKTW* AL2...30 B4
Cricketers Cl *STALW/RED* AL3...........2 E3
Croft Ct *HARP* AL5 * 6 C5
The Croft *LCOL/BKTW* AL2 ....26 B4
Croftwell *HARP* AL5...........13 C1
Cromwell Cl *STALE/WH* AL4...........20 C4
Crosby Cl *STALE/WH* AL4...........28 B2
Crossfields *STALW/RED* AL3...........26 C2
Cross La *HARP* AL5...........12 D4
Crosspaths *HARP* AL5...........5 F2
Cross St *STALW/RED* AL3...........2 C6
Cross Wy *HARP* AL5...........6 D3
Crouch Hall Gdns
  STALW/RED AL3...........10 D3
Crouch Hall La
  STALW/RED AL3...........10 D4
Crown St *STALW/RED* AL3...........11 E4
Cuckmans Dr *LCOL/BKTW* AL2...26 B4
Culver Rd *STAL* AL1...........3 F3
Cumberland Dr
  STALW/RED AL3...........11 E4
Cunningham Av *STAL* AL1...........27 G1
Cunningham Hill Rd *STAL* AL1...27 G1
Curo Pk *LCOL/BKTW* AL2...........31 F2
Cutmore Dr *STALE/WH* AL4 ....29 G1
Cyrils Wy *STAL* AL1...........27 E2

D

Dale Av *STALE/WH* AL4...........8 A1
Dalewood *HARP* AL5...........7 E5
Dalkeith Rd *HARP* AL5...........6 D4
Dalton St *STALW/RED* AL3...........2 C3
Damson Wy *STALE/WH* AL4 ....24 B2
Dane Cl *HARP* AL5...........6 D2
The Danes *LCOL/BKTW* AL2...30 D2
Darblay Cl *STALE/WH* AL4 ....15 E4
Dark La *HARP* AL5...........13 E2
Darley Cft *LCOL/BKTW* AL2 * ...30 C2
Darwin Cl *STALW/RED* AL3 ....19 F5
Davis Ct *STAL* AL1 * 2 E6
Davys Cl *STALE/WH* AL4 ....14 D2
Dawes La *STALE/WH* AL4...........8 C5
Deacon Cl *STAL* AL1...........27 E3
Dean Moore Cl *STAL* AL1 ....2 C7
Dean's Gdns *STALE/WH* AL4...19 H5
The Deerings *HARP* AL5...........12 B5
De Havilland Cl *STALE/WH* AL4...25 H3
Dell Cl *HARP* AL5...........6 D4
Dellcroft Wy *HARP* AL5...........12 B3
Dellfield *HARP* AL5...........23 C5
Dell Ri *LCOL/BKTW* AL2 ....26 C5
The Dell *STAL* AL1...........3 K2
Derwent Rd *HARP* AL5...........5 F2
De Tany Ct *STAL* AL1...........23 E5
Deva Cl *STALW/RED* AL3...........26 B1
Devon Ct *STAL* AL1 * 23 F5
Devonshire Rd *HARP* AL5...........6 C4
Dexter Cl *STAL* AL1...........3 J7
Dickens Cl *STALW/RED* AL3 ....2 C3
Dickinsons Fld *HARP* AL5...........12 D2
Doggetts Wy *STAL* AL1...........26 D1
Dolphin Yd *STAL* AL1 * 2 C6
Dormie Cl *STALW/RED* AL3...........2 A1
Douglas Rd *HARP* AL5...........6 A4
Down Edge *STALW/RED* AL3 ....10 D4
Downedge *STALW/RED* AL3 ....22 C3

Downes Rd *STALE/WH* AL4...........20 A5
Down Green La *STALE/WH* AL4...14 A2
Drakes Dr *STAL* AL1...........28 A2
Driftwood Av *LCOL/BKTW* AL2...26 B5
The Drive *HARP* AL5...........6 B5
  LCOL/BKTW AL2...........27 H4
Drop La *LCOL/BKTW* AL2 ....30 C5
Drovers Wy *STAL* AL1...........2 C5
Dubrae Cl *STALW/RED* AL3...........26 B1
Dunstable Rd *STALW/RED* AL3...4 C5
Dyke La *STALE/WH* AL4 ....14 D2
Dymoke Gn *STALE/WH* AL4...........23 H1

E

Eastbury Ct *STAL* AL1...........3 G3
East Cl *LCOL/BKTW* AL2...........26 C4
Eastcote Dr *HARP* AL5...........13 E3
East Dr *LCOL/BKTW* AL2...........28 A5
  STALE/WH AL4...........24 D3
Eastfield Ct *STALE/WH* AL4 ....24 C1
East La *STALW/RED* AL3...........8 C5
Eastmoor Pk *HARP* AL5...........12 D3
East Mt *STALE/WH* AL4...........8 C5
Eaton Rd *STAL* AL1...........24 A4
Edison Cl *STALE/WH* AL4 ....24 B5
Edmund Beaufort Dr
  STALW/RED AL3...........2 D2
Edward Cl *STAL* AL1...........3 H7
Eleanor Av *STALW/RED* AL3 ....2 C1
Elizabeth Ct *STALE/WH* AL4...........24 C1
Ellis Flds *STALW/RED* AL3...........23 F1
Elliswick Rd *HARP* AL5...........6 C4
Elm Dr *STALE/WH* AL4...........24 B4
Elm Lawn Cl *STAL* AL1...........1 F3
Ely Rd *STAL* AL1...........24 A5
Englehurst *HARP* AL5...........7 E5
Enid Cl *LCOL/BKTW* AL2...........30 A5
Ennerdale Cl *STAL* AL1...........28 A1
Ennis Cl *HARP* AL5...........13 E3
Ermine Cl *STALW/RED* AL3 ....22 B5
Eskdale *LCOL/BKTW* AL2...........33 E1
Essex St *STAL* AL1...........2 E4
Etna Rd *STALW/RED* AL3...........2 C6
Evans Gv *STALE/WH* AL4...........20 B5
Everard Cl *STAL* AL1...........27 E1
Everlasting La *STALW/RED* AL3...2 A3
Executive Pk *STAL* AL1 * 24 A4
Eywood Rd *STAL* AL1...........26 D1

F

Faircross Wy *STAL* AL1...........3 J2
Fairfield Cl *HARP* AL5...........7 E5
Fairhaven *LCOL/BKTW* AL2 * ...31 E1
Fairmead Av *HARP* AL5...........12 D1
Fairway Cl *HARP* AL5...........12 B4
  LCOL/BKTW AL2...........30 D1
Falconers Fld *HARP* AL5...........5 G3
Fallows Gn *HARP* AL5...........6 C3
Falmouth Ct *STALW/RED* AL3...........2 B2
Farm Av *HARP* AL5...........6 C3
Farm Crs *LCOL/BKTW* AL2 ....26 D2
Farm Av *HARP* AL5...........27 H5
Farm Rd *STAL* AL1...........24 A3
Farriday Cl *STALW/RED* AL3 ....19 F5
Farringford Cl *LCOL/BKTW* AL2...26 B5
Ferndene *LCOL/BKTW* AL2...........30 A5
Fernecroft *STAL* AL1...........26 D2
Fernleys *STALE/WH* AL4...........24 B1
Ferrers La *HARP* AL5...........13 C4
  STALE/WH AL4...........14 C4
Field Cl *HARP* AL5...........13 E2
  STALE/WH AL4...........19 H5
Fieldfares *LCOL/BKTW* AL2...........32 C1
Finley Rd *HARP* AL5...........7 E3
Firbank Rd *STALW/RED* AL3...........19 C5
Firs Dr *STALE/WH* AL4...........8 B1
The Firs *HARP* AL5 * 7 E4
  STAL AL1...........28 A3
Firwood Av *STALE/WH* AL4 ....24 D4
Fishpool St *STALW/RED* AL3...........2 B6
Fish St *STALW/RED* AL3...........11 E4
Fish St Farm *STALW/RED* AL3...11 E4
Five Acres *LCOL/BKTW* AL2...........28 C4
Five Acres Av *LCOL/BKTW* AL2...30 A3
Flamsteadbury La
  STALW/RED AL3...........10 D5
Flavian Cl *STALW/RED* AL3 ....26 A1
Flinders Cl *STAL* AL1...........27 H1
Flint Copse *HARP* AL5...........11 F3
Flint Wy *STALW/RED* AL3...........18 D5
Flora Gv *STAL* AL1...........3 H7
Floral Dr *LCOL/BKTW* AL2...........28 C5

Flowton Gv *HARP* AL5...........12 B2
Folly Av *STALW/RED* AL3...........2 B3
Folly Flds *STALW/RED* AL3...........2 A4
Folly La *STALW/RED* AL4...........8 A4
Folly La *STALW/RED* AL3...........2 A4
Fontmell Cl *STALW/RED* AL3...........3 F1
Forefield *LCOL/BKTW* AL2...........30 B1
Forest La *RAD* WD7...........32 A5
Forge End *LCOL/BKTW* AL2...........26 B5
Form Cl *RAD* WD7...........32 D5
Four Limes *STALE/WH* AL4...........14 C1
Fovant Cl *HARP* AL5...........12 D3
Foxcroft *STAL* AL1...........27 H1
Francis Av *STALW/RED* AL3...........23 E1
French Rw *STALW/RED* AL3...........2 C6
Friars Wash *STALW/RED* AL3 * 4 C4
Frobisher Rd *STAL* AL1...........28 B1
Frogmore *LCOL/BKTW* AL2...........31 F1
Fryth Md *STALW/RED* AL3...........22 C3
Fulmore Cl *HARP* AL5...........7 E2
Furse Av *STALE/WH* AL4...........23 H1
Furzedown Ct *HARP* AL5...........12 C1

G

Gainsborough Av *STAL* AL1 ....3 G4
Garden Cl *HARP* AL5...........12 B4
  STAL AL1...........24 A3
Garden Ct *STALE/WH* AL4...........8 C5
Garnett Dr *STALW/RED* AL3...........30 A3
Garrard Wy *STALE/WH* AL4...........14 C1
George St *STALW/RED* AL3...........2 C6
Gertrude Peake Pl
  STALW/RED AL3 * 11 E4
Gibbons Cl *STALE/WH* AL4...........20 B3
Gidian Ct *LCOL/BKTW* AL2...........30 D1
Gilbert Ct *HARP* AL5 * 6 C2
Giles Cl *STALE/WH* AL4...........20 B3
Gillian Av *STAL* AL1...........26 D3
Gilpin Gn *HARP* AL5...........6 D5
Gilsted Ct *STALW/RED* AL3 ....19 E5
Gladeside *STALE/WH* AL4...........24 C1
Gleave Cl *STAL* AL1...........24 A3
Glemsford Dr *HARP* AL5...........7 E4
Glenferrie Rd *STAL* AL1...........3 J5
Glengall Pl *STAL* AL1 * 27 F2
Glenlyn Av *STAL* AL1...........24 A5
Glevum Cl *STALW/RED* AL3 ....26 A1
Globe Cl *HARP* AL5...........6 D5
Goldring Wy *LCOL/BKTW* AL2...28 A5
Goldsmith Wy *STALW/RED* AL3...2 C2
Gombards *STALW/RED* AL3...........2 C6
Gordon Cl *STAL* AL1...........24 A5
Gordons Wk *HARP* AL5...........12 D1
Gorham Dr *STAL* AL1...........27 F2
Gorse Cnr *HARP* AL5...........12 D1
  STALW/RED AL3 * 2 D1
Gorselands *HARP* AL5...........12 C2
Grafton Cl *STALE/WH* AL4...........24 C5
Graham Cl *STAL* AL1...........27 E2
Granary Cl *STALE/WH* AL4...........14 C1
Granary La *HARP* AL5...........6 C5
Granby Av *HARP* AL5...........6 D4
Grange Court Rd *HARP* AL5...12 D3
Grange St *STALW/RED* AL3...........2 D1
Grant Gdns *HARP* AL5...........6 C4
Granville Rd *STAL* AL1...........3 G6
Grasmere Av *HARP* AL5...........6 D4
Grasmere Rd *STAL* AL1...........28 A1
Grassington Cl
  LCOL/BKTW AL2...........30 B4
Greatfield Cl *HARP* AL5...........5 F2
Greenbanks *STAL* AL1...........27 C1
Green La *STAL* AL1...........27 H3
  STALW/RED AL3...........22 D1
Green Lane Cl *HARP* AL5...........13 F1
Greensleeves Cl
  STALW/RED AL3...........24 B5
The Green *LCOL/BKTW* AL2 * ...32 C1
Greenway *HARP* AL5...........13 E1
Grenadier Cl *STALE/WH* AL4...........24 B5
Gresford Cl *STALE/WH* AL4 ....24 C4
Greyfriars La *HARP* AL5...........12 B2
Griffiths Wy *STAL* AL1...........26 D1
Grimston Rd *STAL* AL1...........3 G7
Grimthorpe Cl *STALW/RED* AL3...22 D1
Grindcobbe Cl *STAL* AL1...........27 E2
Grosvenor Rd *STAL* AL1...........3 F7
Grove Av *HARP* AL5...........13 E2
Grovebury Gdns
  LCOL/BKTW AL2...........30 D1
Grovelands *LCOL/BKTW* AL2...30 C1
Grove Rd *HARP* AL5...........13 E2
  STAL AL1...........23 E5
The Grove *HARP* AL5 * 13 F2
Guildford Rd *STAL* AL1...........24 A5
Gurney Court Rd *STAL* AL1...........3 H1
Gustard Wd *STALE/WH* AL4...........8 B2

H

Hadleigh Ct *HARP* AL5...........1
Hadrian Cl *STALW/RED* AL3...........2
Hagi Cl *STAL* AL1...........2
Hales Meadow *HARP* AL5...........6
Half Moon Ms *STAL* AL1...........
Halifax Cl *LCOL/BKTW* AL2...........2
Hall Heath Cl *STAL* AL1...........2
Hall Pl *STAL* AL1 * ....
Hall Place Cl *STAL* AL1...........
Hall Place Gdns *STAL* AL1...........
Halsey Pk *LCOL/BKTW* AL2...........3
Halton Cl *LCOL/BKTW* AL2...........3
Hamilton Cl *LCOL/BKTW* AL2...........3
Hamilton Rd *STAL* AL1...........
Hamlet Cl *STALW/RED* AL3...........3
Hammers Ga *LCOL/BKTW* AL2...........2
Hammond End La *HARP* AL5...........1
Hammonds Hl *HARP* AL5...........1
Hammonds La *HAT* AL10...........2
Hammondswick *HARP* AL5...........1
Hampden Pl *LCOL/BKTW* AL2...........2
Hampstead Cl *LCOL/BKTW* AL2...30
Handley Page Wy
  LCOL/BKTW AL2...........3
Harbert Gdns *LCOL/BKTW* AL2...30
Harding Cl *STALW/RED* AL3...........1
Harding Pde *HARP* AL5 * ....
Hardwicke Pl *LCOL/BKTW* AL2...........3
Harefield Pl *STALE/WH* AL4...........2
Harlesden Rd *STAL* AL1...........
Harley Ct *STALE/WH* AL4 * 20
Harness Wy *STALE/WH* AL4...........
Harpenden La *STALW/RED* AL3...1
Harpenden Ri *HARP* AL5...........
Harpenden Rd *STALE/WH* AL4...........1
  STALW/RED AL3...........1
Harper La *RAD* WD7...........3
Harptree Wy *STAL* AL1...........
Hart Rd *STAL* AL1...........
Hartwell Gdns *HARP* AL5...........
Harvest Ct *STALE/WH* AL4...........20
Harvesters Ms *STALE/WH* AL4 * ...20
Harvey Rd *LCOL/BKTW* AL2...........28
Haseldine Rd *LCOL/BKTW* AL2...28
Haslingden Cl *HARP* AL5...........
Hatching Green Cl *HARP* AL5 ...12
Hatfield Rd *STAL* AL1...........
Hathaway Ct *STALE/WH* AL4 ...24
Havercroft Cl *STALW/RED* AL3 ...26
Hawfield Gdns
  LCOL/BKTW AL2...........27
Hawkes Dr *STALW/RED* AL3...........11
Hawkshill *STAL* AL1...........
Hawsley Rd *HARP* AL5...........12
Hawthorn Cl *HARP* AL5...........13
Hawthorn Wy *LCOL/BKTW* AL2...26
Hay La *HARP* AL5...........
Hazelmere Rd *STALE/WH* AL4 ...24
Hazel Rd *LCOL/BKTW* AL2...........30
Hazelwood Dr *STALE/WH* AL4...........24
Heath Av *STALW/RED* AL3...........
Heath Cl *HARP* AL5...........12
Heath Farm La *STAL* AL1...........2
Heathlands Dr *STALW/RED* AL3 ...2
Heath Rd *STAL* AL1...........
Heathside *STAL* AL1...........3
  STALE/WH AL4...........29
Heath Wy *RAD* WD7...........32
Hedley Rd *STAL* AL1...........26
Hemel Hempstead Rd
  STALW/RED AL3...........16
  STALW/RED AL3...........22
Henderson Cl *STALW/RED* AL3 ...18
Henrys Grant *STAL* AL1...........23
Heracles Cl *LCOL/BKTW* AL2...........30
Heritage Cl *STALW/RED* AL3 * 2
Herons Wy *STAL* AL1...........27
Hewitt Cl *STALE/WH* AL4...........14
Heydons Cl *STALE/WH* AL4...........19
Heyford End *LCOL/BKTW* AL2...30
Hickling Wy *HARP* AL5...........6
High Ash Rd *STALE/WH* AL4 ...14
High Elms *HARP* AL5...........12
Highfield Av *HARP* AL5...........12
Highfield La *STALE/WH* AL4...........6
Highfield Ov *HARP* AL5...........6
Highfield Park Dr
  STALE/WH AL4...........28
Highfield Rd *STALE/WH* AL4...........28
High Firs Crs *HARP* AL5...........13
High Gv *STALW/RED* AL3...........2
High Meads *STALE/WH* AL4...........14
Highmoor *HARP* AL5...........6
High Oaks *STALW/RED* AL3...........18
High Rdg *HARP* AL5...........

h St HARP AL5....................6 B5
COL/BKTW AL2..............28 B4
TALE/WH AL4....................8 C5
TALW/RED AL3.................20 A3
TALW/RED AL3.................29 H1
bs CI STALE/WH AL4.........11 E4
hview Gdns STALE/WH AL4...20 B4
CI HARP AL5......................6 D2
crest STALW/RED AL3 *.....26 A5
Dyke Rd STALE/WH AL4....14 D2
End La STAL AL1...............28 B2
TALE/WH AL4...................24 C5
Farm La STALW/RED AL3...17 F3
VLYN AL6..........................9 H2
side Rd HARP AL5..............6 A3
TAL AL1.............................3 F4
St STALW/RED AL3.............2 A5
Hill STALE/WH AL4...........14 C1
top STALW/RED AL3.........10 D3
top Wk HARP AL5.............13 E1
erfield La HARP AL5............6 E4
art Wk STALW/RED AL3....19 C5
bs CI STALE/WH AL4.........24 D5
born CI STALE/WH AL4.....20 C4
croft Rd HARP AL5..............7 E5
Hollies STAL AL1 *.............2 E5
lybush Av LCOL/BKTW AL2..26 B4
lybush La HARP AL5............6 B3
ly Wk HARP AL5..................7 E5
ts Meadow HARP AL5.........10 D3
yrood Crs STAL AL1............27 E3
ywell HI STAL AL1..............23 E5
nestead CI LCOL/BKTW AL2..30 D1
newood Rd STAL AL1.........24 A1
eycroft Dr STALE/WH AL4..28 B2
oground CI STAL AL1.........27 H1
okins Crs STAL AL1..............2 E7
okins Yd STAL AL1...............2 E7
rdle Gdns STAL AL1............23 C5
nbeams LCOL/BKTW AL2....30 A4
semans Dr LCOL/BKTW AL2..26 B5
usden CI STALE/WH AL4....14 D2
usefield Wy STALE/WH AL4..28 B2
use La STALE/WH AL4.........20 C4
use La STAL AL1................28 B2
w Fld HARP AL5..................5 H3
wland Garth STAL AL1.......26 D3
w Wd LCOL/BKTW AL2......30 D1
dson CI STAL AL1..............26 D2
ghenden Rd STALE/WH AL4..24 A1
nt CI STALE/WH AL4..........24 C1
nters Ride LCOL/BKTW AL2..30 B5
burn CI LCOL/BKTW AL2....30 A4
de CI HARP AL5...................6 C2
de La LCOL/BKTW AL2.......31 F2
de View Rd HARP AL5.........6 C2

I

nield CI STALW/RED AL3.....26 A1
lewood Gdns
COL/BKTW AL2...............27 G4
erman Rd STAL AL1.............2 E7
ghoe CI STALE/WH AL4......20 B4
ry CI STALE/WH AL4..........28 B2

J

neson Rd HARP AL5.............6 C3
nings Rd STAL AL1...............3 J3
ome Dr STALW/RED AL3....26 B1
sey La STAL AL1................24 A2
STALE/WH AL4..................20 B3
ilee Av LCOL/BKTW AL2....28 C5
iper Av LCOL/BKTW AL2....30 B5

K

y Wk STALE/WH AL4..........24 C1
mpe CI STAL AL1...............26 D3
nnedy CI LCOL/BKTW AL2..28 C5
nnel La HARP AL5................4 D1
nsington CI STAL AL1.........27 H1
nton Gdns STAL AL1...........23 C5
e Kestrels LCOL/BKTW AL2..30 A4
swick CI STAL AL1..............28 A1
yfield STAL AL1...................2 D7
nberley Rd STALW/RED AL3..2 B3
g Croft Rd HARP AL5.........13 C2
g Edward PI STALE/WH AL4....8 C5
gfisher La HARP AL5............8 C5
g Harry La STALW/RED AL3..26 C1

Kingsbury Av STALW/RED AL3....2 A4
Kingsgate STALW/RED AL3..26 C1
Kingshill Av STAL AL1.........24 A1
Kingsmead STALE/WH AL4..24 C1
King's Rd LCOL/BKTW AL2....28 B5
STALW/RED AL3..............22 C3
Kinsbourne CI HARP AL5.......5 F2
Kinsbourne Crs HARP AL5.....5 G2
Kinsbourne Green La HARP AL5....5 E5
Kipling Wy HARP AL5............6 C5
Kirkdale Rd HARP AL5...........6 B5
Kirkwick Av HARP AL5...........6 B5
Kitchener CI STAL AL1.........23 H5
Knights Orch STALW/RED AL3....2 A5
Knowle Dr HARP AL5...........13 E2

L

Laburnum Gv LCOL/BKTW AL2..26 B4
Ladies Gv STALW/RED AL3...22 C3
Ladysmith Rd STALW/RED AL3....2 C3
Lakeside PI LCOL/BKTW AL2..32 C2
Lamb Ct STALE/WH AL4 *....14 D2
Lamb La STALW/RED AL3.....11 E4
Lambourn Gdns HARP AL5......6 A3
Lamer La STALE/WH AL4.......8 C2
Lancaster Rd STAL AL1..........3 H2
Langdale Av HARP AL5...........7 H4
Langford CI STALE/WH AL4..20 B4
Langham CI STALE/WH AL4..20 B4
Langley Crs STALW/RED AL3..2 B1
Langley Gv STALW/RED AL3..20 B2
The Larches STALE/WH AL4..20 C5
Larks Rdg LCOL/BKTW AL2...26 B5
Larkswood Ri STALE/WH AL4..20 C5
Latchford Ms STALE/WH AL4....8 C5
Latium Ct STAL AL1.............23 C5
Lattimore Rd STAL AL1..........2 E7
STALE/WH AL4..................14 B1
Laurel Rd STAL AL1...............3 H5
Laurels CI STALW/RED AL3...26 C2
Lavender Crs STALE/WH AL4...2 B1
The Lawns STALW/RED AL3....2 A4
Lawrance Rd STALE/WH AL4..18 D5
Lay Brook STALE/WH AL4.....19 H5
Lea Rd HARP AL5...................6 D3
Leasey Bridge La HARP AL5....7 G5
Leasey Dell Dr STALE/WH AL4..7 H4
Lea Wk HARP AL5.................6 D2
Lectern La STAL AL1..............3 G4
Lemsford Rd STAL AL1...........3 G4
Leycroft Wy STALE/WH AL4....6 B2
Leyland Av STAL AL1............27 E1
The Leys STALE/WH AL4.......24 C1
Leyton Gn HARP AL5.............6 B5
Leyton Rd HARP AL5..............6 B5
Liberty Wk STAL AL1............28 B1
Lichfield PI STAL AL1 *...........3 G3
Lilac Wy HARP AL5...............13 E3
Lilly La HHNE HP2...............16 A5
Limbrick Rd HARP AL5.........12 C3
The Limes STAL AL1..............2 E2
Lime Tree Ct LCOL/BKTW AL2..28 A5
Lime Tree PI STAL AL1............3 G7
Lime Wy RAD WD7..............32 B4
Lincoln's Av STALE/WH AL4..20 A4
Linden Ct HARP AL5.............20 A4
Linden Crs STAL AL1............24 B4
Linden Rd STALW/RED AL3...10 D3
Lindley CI HARP AL5..............6 B2
Lindum PI STALW/RED AL3...26 B1
Links Vw STALW/RED AL3.....22 C2
Linwood Rd HARP AL5..........12 D2
Little Acre STALW/RED AL3...18 D5
Little La HARP AL5................12 D3
Liverpool Rd STAL AL1...........2 E6
Lodge Gdns HARP AL5............6 B5
London Rd STAL AL1.............27 H2
Longacres STALE/WH AL4.....24 C4
Long Buftlers HARP AL5........13 C1
Longcroft Av HARP AL5..........6 A5
Long Cutt STALW/RED AL3....2 A5
Long Fallow LCOL/BKTW AL2..30 B1
Longfield Rd HARP AL5.........12 D2
Long Spring STALW/RED AL3..19 G5
Lords Meadow STALW/RED AL3..10 B4
Lovett Rd LCOL/BKTW AL2....27 H5
Lowbell La LCOL/BKTW AL2..32 D1
Lower Dagnall St
STALW/RED AL3...................2 B5
Lower Luton Rd HARP AL5.....6 C1
Lower Paxton Rd STAL AL1....2 E7
STAL AL1.............................23 F5
Luton La STALW/RED AL3.....10 D1
Luton Rd HARP AL5................5 F1
Lybury La STALW/RED AL3...10 D3
Lycaste CI STAL AL1...............3 H7

Lye La LCOL/BKTW AL2........30 B2
Lyndhurst CI HARP AL5..........6 D4
Lyndhurst Dr HARP AL5.........6 D4
Lyndon Md STALE/WH AL4..20 B2
Lynsey CI STALW/RED AL3....10 D3
Lynton Av STAL AL1..............28 B1
Lyon Wy STALE/WH AL4.......25 F4

M

Magna CI HARP AL5..............13 E3
Magnolia CI LCOL/BKTW AL2..27 E5
Maldon Ct HARP AL5.............6 C4
The Mall LCOL/BKTW AL2....30 D1
Maltings Dr STALE/WH AL4..14 B2
Malvern CI STALE/WH AL4....20 A5
Mandeville Dr STAL AL1.......27 E2
Manland Av HARP AL5...........6 D4
Manland Wy STALE/WH AL4...6 D4
Manor Dr LCOL/BKTW AL2...30 B1
Manor Rd LCOL/BKTW AL2...28 B5
STAL AL1..............................3 F4
STALE/WH AL4......................7 A4
Mansdale Rd STALW/RED AL3..10 C5
Manston Wy STALE/WH AL4..24 C5
Maple Av STALW/RED AL3...18 D5
Maplefield LCOL/BKTW AL2..30 D3
Maple Rd HARP AL5................6 A5
Marconi Wy STALE/WH AL4..24 C4
Marford Rd STALE/WH AL4...15 F1
Margaret Av STALW/RED AL3..2 C1
Market PI HARP AL5................2 C6
Marlborough Ga STAL AL1......2 C6
Marlborough Pk HARP AL5....12 D2
Marlborough Rd STAL AL1......7 A4
Marquis CI HARP AL5..............7 A4
Marquis La HARP AL5.............7 A4
Marshall Av STALW/RED AL3..23 F1
Marshalls Heath La HARP AL5..7 H2
Marshalls Wy STALE/WH AL4..7 A4
Marshal's Dr STAL AL1..........23 H1
Marshalswick La STAL AL1....23 H1
Marten Ga STALE/WH AL4....19 H5
Martyr CI STAL AL1...............27 E3
Masefield Ct HARP AL5...........6 C2
Masefield Rd HARP AL5..........6 C2
Maxwell Rd STAL AL1...........24 A5
May CI STALW/RED AL3..........2 A5
Mayfair CI STALE/WH AL4....20 B4
Mayfield CI HARP AL5.............5 H3
Mayflower Rd LCOL/BKTW AL2..30 C1
Maynard Dr STAL AL1...........27 E2
Mayne Av STALW/RED AL3...22 B5
Meadow Av RAD WD7..........32 B5
Meadow CI LCOL/BKTW AL2 *....30 B4
LCOL/BKTW AL2.................32 C1
RAD WD7............................32 B4
STALE/WH AL4...................24 B1
Meadowcroft STAL AL1.........27 H3
The Meadow STALW/RED AL3 *..11 E4
Meadow Wk HARP AL5.........12 D1
Meads La STALE/WH AL4........8 C5
The Meads LCOL/BKTW AL2..30 A3
Meadway HARP AL5..............13 F2
Meautys STALW/RED AL3.....26 A1
Medlows HARP AL5................5 H4
Melbourne CI STALW/RED AL3..19 G5
Mendip CI STALE/WH AL4....20 B4
Mentmore Rd STAL AL1.........27 F1
Mercers Rw STAL AL1............26 D1
Merryfields STALE/WH AL4...24 D4
The Mews HARP AL5 *............6 C5
Middlefield CI STALE/WH AL4..24 B1
Midway STALW/RED AL3......26 C2
Mile House CI STAL AL1........27 H2
Mile House La STAL AL1........27 H2
Milford CI STALE/WH AL4.....20 C5
Milford HI HARP AL5..............7 E3
Miller CI STALW/RED AL3.....11 E4
Millers Ri STAL AL1...............23 F5
Milliners Ct STAL AL1 *...........2 E6
Milton Rd HARP AL5.............12 D1
Minister Ct LCOL/BKTW AL2..31 F2
Mitchell CI STAL AL1.............27 E3
Molescroft HARP AL5..............5 G2
Monastery CI STALW/RED AL3..27 F1
Monks CI STAL AL1...............27 F1
STALW/RED AL3...................11 E4
Monks Horton Wy STAL AL1....3 K2
Mons CI HARP AL5................13 E3
Moorland Rd HARP AL5..........6 C4
Moorlands LCOL/BKTW AL2 *..31 F2
Moor Mill La STALW/RED AL3..31 F4
Moran CI LCOL/BKTW AL2....30 A5
Moreton Av HARP AL5............6 A4
Moreton End CI HARP AL5......6 A4
Moreton End La HARP AL5......6 A4

Moreton PI HARP AL5.............6 A3
Morris Wy LCOL/BKTW AL2..28 C5
Moss Side LCOL/BKTW AL2...30 A4
Mountbatten CI STAL AL1.....28 C5
Mount Dr LCOL/BKTW AL2....28 C5
Mount Pleasant STALW/RED AL3..2 A5
Mount Pleasant La
LCOL/BKTW AL2.................30 A4
Mount Rd STALE/WH AL4.......8 C5
Mount Vw LCOL/BKTW AL2..32 D1
Mulberry CI LCOL/BKTW AL2..30 C2
Mulberry PI STALW/RED AL3 *..11 E5
Murton Ct STAL AL1...............3 F4

N

Nairn CI HARP AL5................13 E3
Napier CI LCOL/BKTW AL2....28 C4
Napsbury Av HARP AL5.........28 B5
Napsbury La STAL AL1..........27 H2
Necton Rd STALE/WH AL4....14 D1
Nelson Av STAL AL1..............28 A2
Netherfield Rd HARP AL5......12 C5
Netherway STALW/RED AL3..26 B2
New Barnes Av STAL AL1......27 H2
New England St
STALW/RED AL3.....................2 B5
New Fiddlers HI HARP AL5 *....5 F1
Newfield Wy STALE/WH AL4...4 B2
Newgate CI STALE/WH AL4...24 D1
New Greens Av
STALW/RED AL3...................19 E5
New House Pk STAL AL1.......27 H2
Newland CI STAL AL1............27 H2
Newmans Dr HARP AL5..........6 A4
Newmarket Ct STALW/RED AL3..2 B3
Newton CI HARP AL5.............13 E3
Nicholas CI STALW/RED AL3..23 E1
Nicholls CI STALW/RED AL3...10 C4
Nicky Line STALW/RED AL3...16 B3
Nightingale La STAL AL1........28 B3
Nimrod CI STALW/RED AL3...24 A2
Ninnings Cottages HARP AL5 *..12 B1
Noke Shot HARP AL5..............6 D2
Noke Side LCOL/BKTW AL2...30 B1
Norman CI STAL AL1.............27 F2
Normandy Rd STALW/RED AL3..2 C3
Norris CI LCOL/BKTW AL2.....28 C5
North CI LCOL/BKTW AL2.....26 C4
North Common Rd
STALW/RED AL3...................10 D5
North Dr STALE/WH AL4.......24 D2
Northfield Rd HARP AL5.........6 D2
North Orbital Rd
LCOL/BKTW AL2.................30 B1
North Riding LCOL/BKTW AL2..30 B4
Nunnery CI STAL AL1............27 F1
Nunnery Stables STAL AL1....27 E1
Nuns La STAL AL1................27 F3
Nurseries Rd STALE/WH AL4..14 D2

O

Oak Av LCOL/BKTW AL2.......30 B4
Oakdene Wy STAL AL1..........24 B4
Oakfield Rd HARP AL5...........12 B4
Oakhurst Av HARP AL5..........12 A4
Oaklands La STALE/WH AL4..25 E2
Oakley Rd HARP AL5.............13 E2
Oakridge LCOL/BKTW AL2....30 A3
Oakview CI HARP AL5...........12 A4
Oak Wy HARP AL5...............12 A4
Oakwood Dr HARP AL5.........12 A4
STALE/WH AL4....................24 B3
Oakwood Rd LCOL/BKTW AL2..30 A3
Offa Rd STALW/RED AL3.......14 C1
Offas Wy STALE/WH AL4......14 C1
Oldfield Rd LCOL/BKTW AL2..28 C4
Old Garden Ct STALW/RED AL3..2 B5
Old Harpenden Rd
STALW/RED AL3...................19 F5
Old London Rd STAL AL1........2 D7
Old Oak STAL AL1................27 F2
Old Orch LCOL/BKTW AL2....27 E5
Old Parkbury La
LCOL/BKTW AL2.................31 G4
Old Rectory CI HARP AL5.......6 B4
Old Rectory Gdns
STALE/WH AL4......................8 C5
Old Sopwell Gdns STAL AL1..27 F1
Olive CI STAL AL1................24 A5
Oliver CI LCOL/BKTW AL2....31 E1
Orchard Av HARP AL5.............6 A5
Orchard CI STAL AL1.............23 C5
Orchard Dr LCOL/BKTW AL2..26 C4

Orchard House La *STAL* AL1 ....2 C7
Orchard St *STALW/RED* AL3 ....2 B7
Orient Cl *STAL* AL1 ....27 G1
Orton Cl *STALE/WH* AL4 ....19 H5
Oster St *STALW/RED* AL3 ....2 B4
Oswald Rd *STAL* AL1 ....3 F7
Otterton Ct *HARP* AL5 ....6 A3
Oulton Ri *HARP* AL5 ....6 D3
Overstone Rd *HARP* AL5 ....6 D5
Oxford Av *STAL* AL1 ....24 B5
Ox La *HARP* AL5 ....6 C3
Oysterfields *STALW/RED* AL3 ....2 A3

P

Packhorse Cl *STALE/WH* AL4 ....24 B1
The Paddocks
   STALE/WH AL4 * 29 G1
Paddock Wd *HARP* AL5 ....13 F2
Pageant Rd *STAL* AL1 ....2 D7
Palfrey Cl *STALW/RED* AL3 ....2 D2
Palmerston Dr *STALE/WH* AL4 ....8 C5
Park Av *STAL* AL1 ....3 J4
Park Av North *HARP* AL5 ....6 A5
Park Av South *HARP* AL5 ....5 H5
Park Hl *HARP* AL5 ....6 A4
Parkinson Cl *STALE/WH* AL4 ....14 C1
Parklands Dr *STALW/RED* AL3 ....22 B5
Park La *STALE/WH* AL4 ....29 H2
Park Mt *HARP* AL5 ....5 H4
Park Pl *LCOL/BKTW* AL2 ....31 E1
Park Ri *HARP* AL5 ....5 H3
Park Rise Cl *HARP* AL5 ....5 H3
Park St *LCOL/BKTW* AL2 ....31 E1
Park Street La
   LCOL/BKTW AL2 ....30 C3
The Park *STAL* AL1 ....3 K1
   STALW/RED AL3 ....11 H3
Park View Cl *STAL* AL1 ....3 K7
Parkway Ct *STAL* AL1 ....28 A2
Partridge Rd *STALW/RED* AL3 ....19 E5
Parva Cl *HARP* AL5 ....13 E3
The Pastures *LCOL/BKTW* AL2 ....26 B3
Paxton Rd *STAL* AL1 ....2 E7
Peakes Pl *STAL* AL1 * 3 G6
Pearces Wk *STAL* AL1 ....2 D7
Pegasus Pl *STALW/RED* AL3 ....2 C5
Pegrum Dr *LCOL/BKTW* AL2 ....32 A1
Pemberton Cl *STAL* AL1 ....27 E2
Pendennis Ct *HARP* AL5 ....13 E2
Penman Cl *LCOL/BKTW* AL2 ....30 B1
Penn Rd *LCOL/BKTW* AL2 ....30 D1
Penny Cft *HARP* AL5 ....12 B5
Penshurst Cl *HARP* AL5 ....5 G2
Peppard Cl *STALW/RED* AL3 ....10 D3
Perham Wy *LCOL/BKTW* AL2 ....28 C5
Peters Av *LCOL/BKTW* AL2 ....28 B5
Petersfield *STALW/RED* AL3 ....19 F5
Pickford Hl *HARP* AL5 ....6 D3
Pigeonwick *HARP* AL5 ....13 D2
Piggottshill La *HARP* AL5 ....12 D2
Pikes Leap *STALE/WH* AL4 ....8 C5
Pilgrim Cl *LCOL/BKTW* AL2 ....30 D1
Pine Gv *LCOL/BKTW* AL2 ....30 A4
Pine Rdg *STAL* AL1 * 27 H2
Pinewood Cl *STALE/WH* AL4 ....24 B4
Pipers Av *HARP* AL5 ....13 E2
Pipers Cl *STALW/RED* AL3 ....10 D3
Pipers La *HARP* AL5 ....13 F2
Pirton Cl *STALE/WH* AL4 ....20 B4
Pitstone Cl *STALE/WH* AL4 ....20 B4
Pitt Dr *STALE/WH* AL4 ....28 B2
The Pleasance *HARP* AL5 ....5 G2
Poets Ct *HARP* AL5 ....6 C5
Pondfield Crs *STALE/WH* AL4 ....24 A1
Pondsmeade *STALW/RED* AL3 ....11 E4
Pondwick Rd *HARP* AL5 ....5 H4
Pondwicks Cl *STAL* AL1 ....2 D7
The Poplars *STAL* AL1 ....28 A3
Porters Hl *HARP* AL5 ....6 D2
Porters Wd *STALW/RED* AL3 ....19 G5
Portland St *STALW/RED* AL3 ....2 A4
Portman Cl *STALE/WH* AL4 ....20 B4
Potters Fld *STALW/RED* AL3 ....19 F5
Pound Cl *STALE/WH* AL4 * 20 B2
Poynings Cl *HARP* AL5 ....13 G1
Prae Cl *STALW/RED* AL3 ....22 C3
Praetorian Cl *STAL* AL1 ....26 D2
Princess Diana Dr
   STALW/RED AL3 ....28 B1
The Priory *STALW/RED* AL3 * 11 E4
Priory Wk *STAL* AL1 ....27 F2
Prospect La *HARP* AL5 ....12 A5
Prospect Rd *STAL* AL1 ....27 E1
Puddingstone Dr
   STALE/WH AL4 ....28 B1
Pullman Cl *STAL* AL1 ....27 F1

Punch Bowl La
   STALW/RED AL3 ....16 D5

Q

The Quadrant *STALE/WH* AL4 ....24 A1
Quantock Cl *STALE/WH* AL4 ....20 B5
Queens Crs *STALE/WH* AL4 ....24 A1
Queens Rd *HARP* AL5 ....12 C2
Queen St *STALW/RED* AL3 ....2 B6
Queens Wy *RAD* WD7 ....32 D5

R

Radlett Rd *LCOL/BKTW* AL2 ....31 F3
Ragged Hall La *LCOL/BKTW* AL2 ...26 B3
Rainbow Ct *STALW/RED* AL3 ....10 C4
The Ramparts *STALW/RED* AL3 ....26 C1
Ramsbury Rd *STAL* AL1 ....23 F5
Ramsey Cl *STAL* AL1 ....27 H1
Ramsey Lodge Ct *STAL* AL1 * 3 F4
Randalls Wk *LCOL/BKTW* AL2 ....30 A5
Ranleigh Wk *HARP* AL5 ....13 E3
Ravenscroft *HARP* AL5 ....13 E3
Raymer Cl *STAL* AL1 ....3 F3
Rectory La *RAD* WD7 ....33 H5
Redbournbury La
   STALW/RED AL3 ....17 G2
Redbourn La *HARP* AL5 ....11 H3
Redbourn Rd *STALW/RED* AL3 ....17 H5
Redcote La *HARP* AL5 ....12 B2
Redding La *STALW/RED* AL3 ....4 B5
Redfield Cl *STALW/RED* AL3 ....10 D4
Reed Cl *LCOL/BKTW* AL2 ....32 C1
Reedham Cl *LCOL/BKTW* AL2 ....30 B4
Reed Pl *HARP* AL5 * 6 A3
Regent Cl *STALE/WH* AL4 ....20 B5
Remus Cl *STAL* AL1 ....27 E3
Repton Gn *STALW/RED* AL3 ....23 E1
Reynard's Wy *LCOL/BKTW* AL2 .....30 A3
Reynolds Cl *STALW/RED* AL3 ....20 A4
Ribbledale *LCOL/BKTW* AL2 ....33 E1
Richardson Cl
   LCOL/BKTW AL2 ....32 D1
Richardson Pl *STALE/WH* AL4 ....29 G1
Richard Stagg Cl *STAL* AL1 ....28 B1
Richmond Wk *S*
   STALE/WH AL4 ....20 C5
Rickyard Meadow
   STALW/RED AL3 ....10 D4
Ridge Av *HARP* AL5 ....5 H2
Ridgedown *STALW/RED* AL3 ....10 D4
Ridgeview *LCOL/BKTW* AL2 ....33 E2
Ridgeway *HARP* AL5 * 5 H2
   RAD WD7 ....32 B5
The Ridgeway *STALE/WH* AL4 ....24 B1
Ridgeway Dr *HARP* AL5 ....5 H3
Ridgewood Gdns *HARP* AL5 ....5 H2
Ridgmont Rd *STAL* AL1 ....3 F7
Ringway Rd *LCOL/BKTW* AL2 ....30 C2
Ripon Wy *STALE/WH* AL4 ....20 C5
The Rise *LCOL/BKTW* AL2 ....27 E4
Riverbanks Cl *HARP* AL5 ....6 D2
Riverford Cl *HARP* AL5 ....6 C2
Riverside *LCOL/BKTW* AL2 ....32 D1
Riverside Cl *STAL* AL1 ....27 F1
Riverside Rd *STAL* AL1 ....23 F5
Robert Av *STAL* AL1 ....26 D3
Robin Ct *HARP* AL5 * 6 C2
Robins Cl *LCOL/BKTW* AL2 ....32 D1
Rodney Av *STAL* AL1 ....27 H1
Roland St *STAL* AL1 ....3 K6
Romans End *STALW/RED* AL3 ....26 D1
Romeland *STALW/RED* AL3 ....2 B6
Romeland Hl *STALW/RED* AL3 ....2 B6
Ronsons Wy *STALE/WH* AL4 ....19 G5
Rose Acre *STALW/RED* AL3 ....10 C4
Rosebery Av *HARP* AL5 ....6 A4
Rose La *STALE/WH* AL4 ....8 B4
Rosemary Dr *LCOL/BKTW* AL2 ....27 H5
Rose Wk *STALW/RED* AL3 ....6 A5
Rothamsted Av *HARP* AL5 ....7 E2
Roundfield Av *HARP* AL5 ....7 E2
Roundwood Gdns *HARP* AL5 ....5 H4
Roundwood La *HARP* AL5 ....5 E3
Roundwood Pk *HARP* AL5 ....5 H3
Rowan Cl *LCOL/BKTW* AL2 ....30 B5
   STALW/RED AL3 ....24 D4
Rowan Wy *HARP* AL5 ....12 D1
Rowlatt Dr *STALW/RED* AL3 ....26 B1
Royal Rd *STAL* AL1 ....24 A4
Royston Rd *STAL* AL1 ....24 A5
The Ruins *STALW/RED* AL3 ....11 E4
Runcie Cl *STALE/WH* AL4 ....19 H5
Ruscombe Dr *LCOL/BKTW* AL2 ......26 C5

Russell Av *STALW/RED* AL3 ....2 C5
Russet Dr *STALE/WH* AL4 ....28 B1
Ryder Seed Ms *STAL* AL1 * 2 D7
Rye Cl *HARP* AL5 ....6 C2
Rye Hl *HARP* AL5 ....6 C2

S

Saberton Cl *STALW/RED* AL3 ....10 C5
Sadleir Rd *STAL* AL1 ....27 F1
St Albans Rd *HARP* AL5 ....12 C3
   STALE/WH AL4 ....19 H5
   STALW/RED AL3 ....11 F5
St Albans Rd West *HAT* AL10 ....25 H2
St Andrew's Av *HARP* AL5 ....6 A5
St Annes Rd *LCOL/BKTW* AL2 ....32 C1
St Augusta Ct *STALW/RED* AL3 ....2 C1
St Bernard's Rd *STALW/RED* AL3 ....2 E3
St Edmunds Wk *STALE/WH* AL4 ....24 C5
St Helen's Cl *STALE/WH* AL4 ....14 C1
St Heliers Rd *STALE/WH* AL4 ....20 A4
St James Ct *HARP* AL5 * 6 A4
St James Rd *HARP* AL5 ....6 A5
St John's Ct *HARP* AL5 * 12 D2
   STAL AL1 ....24 A3
St Johns Rd *STALW/RED* AL3 ....12 D2
St Julian's Rd *STAL* AL1 ....27 E1
St Lawrence Wy
   LCOL/BKTW AL2 ....30 A4
St Leonard's Ct *STALE/WH* AL4 ......20 B3
St Leonards Crs *STALE/WH* AL4 ......20 B3
St Lukes Pl *STAL* AL1 * 24 A5
St Marks Cl *HARP* AL5 ....29 G1
St Martins Cl *HARP* AL5 ....6 B2
St Mary's Cl *STALW/RED* AL3 ....10 D4
St Marys Wk *STALW/RED* AL3 ....2 D4
St Michaels Cl *HARP* AL5 ....13 E2
St Michael's St *STALW/RED* AL3 ....22 C4
St Pauls Pl *STAL* AL1 ....3 J5
St Peter's Cl *STAL* AL1 ....2 D4
St Peter's Rd *STAL* AL1 ....2 E5
St Peter's St *STAL* AL1 ....2 E4
St Stephen's Av
   STALW/RED AL3 ....26 C2
St Stephen's Cl *STALW/RED* AL3 ....26 C2
St Stephen's Hl *STALW/RED* AL3 ....26 D1
St Thomas Pl *STALE/WH* AL4 ....14 C1
St Vincent Dr *STAL* AL1 ....27 H1
St Yon Ct *STALE/WH* AL4 ....24 C4
Salisbury Av *HARP* AL5 ....6 A4
   STAL AL1 ....24 A4
Salisbury Rd *HARP* AL5 ....7 E3
Samian Ga *STALW/RED* AL3 ....26 A1
Samuel Sq *STAL* AL1 * 2 C7
Sanders Cl *LCOL/BKTW* AL2 ....32 C1
Sandfield Rd *STAL* AL1 ....3 K5
Sandhurst Ct *HARP* AL5 ....13 E3
Sandpit La *STAL* AL1 ....3 F3
Sandridgebury La
   STALW/RED AL3 ....19 F5
Sandridge Pk *STALW/RED* AL3 * ...19 G4
Sandridge Rd *STAL* AL1 ....3 F2
Sandringham Crs
   STALE/WH AL4 ....19 H5
Sauncey Av *HARP* AL5 ....6 C4
Sauncey Wd *HARP* AL5 ....7 E2
Sauncey Wood La *HARP* AL5 ....7 F1
Saxon Cl *HARP* AL5 ....6 D2
Saxon Rd *STALE/WH* AL4 ....14 C2
Seaman Cl *LCOL/BKTW* AL2 ....27 E4
Seaton Rd *LCOL/BKTW* AL2 ....32 C1
Sefton Cl *STAL* AL1 ....3 H3
Selby Av *STALW/RED* AL3 ....2 C5
Severnvale *LCOL/BKTW* AL2 * 33 E1
Sewell Cl *STALE/WH* AL4 ....24 D4
Seymour Rd *STALE/WH* AL4 ....23 F1
Shakespeare Rd *HARP* AL5 ....6 C5
Sheepcote La *STALE/WH* AL4 ....14 D1
Shenleybury *RAD* WD7 ....32 D4
Shenleybury Cottages
   RAD WD7 ....32 D5
Shenley La *LCOL/BKTW* AL2 ....32 B2
Shepherds Wy *HARP* AL5 ....5 G2
Sheppards Cl *STALW/RED* AL3 ....23 F1
Sherwood Av *STALE/WH* AL4 ....24 A1
Sherwoods Ri *HARP* AL5 ....13 E1
Shirley Rd *STAL* AL1 ....3 G7
Shottfield Cl *STALE/WH* AL4 ....20 B4
The Shrubberies *STAL* AL1 * 27 E1
Sibley Av *STAL* AL1 ....13 E2
Siding Wy *LCOL/BKTW* AL2 ....32 C4
Silk Mill Rd *STALW/RED* AL3 ....11 E5
Silver Trees *LCOL/BKTW* AL2 ....30 A4
Sir Joseph's Wk *HARP* AL5 ....12 B1
Skys Wood Rd *STALE/WH* AL4 ....20 A5
Sleapcross Gdns *STALE/WH* AL4 ....25 H5
Sleapshyde La *STALE/WH* AL4 ....25 H5
Slimmons Dr *STALE/WH* AL4 ....19 H5

Slowmans Cl *LCOL/BKTW* AL2 30
The Slype *STALE/WH* AL4 7
Smallford La *STALE/WH* AL4 25
Smallwood Cl *STALE/WH* AL4 14
Smug Oak La *LCOL/BKTW* AL2 30
Snatchup *STALW/RED* AL3 10
Someries Rd *HARP* AL5 6
Soothouse Spring
   STALW/RED AL3 19
Sopwell La *STAL* AL1 2
South Cl *LCOL/BKTW* AL2 26
Southdown Rd *STALW/RED* AL3 12
South Dr *STALE/WH* AL4 24
Southfield Wy *STALE/WH* AL4 24
South Riding *LCOL/BKTW* AL2 6
Southview Rd *HARP* AL5 6
Sovereign Pk *STALE/WH* AL4 6
Sparrowswick Ride
   STALW/RED AL3 18
Spencer Ga *STAL* AL1 2
Spencer Pl *STALW/RED* AL3 20
Spencer St *STALW/RED* AL3 2
Spenser Rd *HARP* AL5 6
Spicer St *STALW/RED* AL3 2
Spinneys Dr *STALW/RED* AL3 * 26
The Spinney *HARP* AL5 5
Spooners Dr *LCOL/BKTW* AL2 30
Springfield Crs *HARP* AL5 6
Springfield Rd *STAL* AL1 23
   STALE/WH AL4 25
Spring Rd *HARP* AL5 4
Springwood Wk *STALE/WH* AL4 4
Spruce Wy *LCOL/BKTW* AL2 30
The Square *STALW/RED* AL3 10
Stakers Ct *HARP* AL5 6
Stanhope Rd *STAL* AL1 3
Stanley Av *LCOL/BKTW* AL2 26
Stanmore Cha *STALE/WH* AL4 24
Stanmount Rd
   LCOL/BKTW AL2 * 20
Stanton Cl *STALE/WH* AL4 20
Stapley Rd *STALW/RED* AL3 2
Starlight Wy *STALE/WH* AL4 28
Station Ap *HARP* AL5 6
Station Rd *HARP* AL5 6
   LCOL/BKTW AL2 30
   STALE/WH AL4.............................6
Station Wy *STAL* AL1 3
Stephens Wy *STALW/RED* AL3 10
Stewart Rd *HARP* AL5 6
Stonecross *STAL* AL1 2
Stonemason Cl *HARP* AL5 6
Stratford Wy *LCOL/BKTW* AL2 30
Strawberry Crs *LCOL/BKTW* AL2 28
Sturmer Cl *STALE/WH* AL4 24
Suffolk Cl *LCOL/BKTW* AL2 28
Summerfield Cl *LCOL/BKTW* AL2 28
Summerhill Ct *STAL* AL1 * 6
Summersland Rd
   STALE/WH AL4 20
Summers Wy *LCOL/BKTW* AL2 * 32
Sumpter Yd *STAL* AL1 2
Sunderland Av *STAL* AL1 3
Sun La *HARP* AL5 6
Sunnydell *LCOL/BKTW* AL2 26
Sutton Rd *STAL* AL1 24
Swallow La *STAL* AL1 28
Swans Cl *STALE/WH* AL4 24
Sycamore Dr *LCOL/BKTW* AL2 31

T

Tallents Crs *HARP* AL5 7
Tamarisk Cl *STALW/RED* AL3 19
Tankerfield Pl *STALW/RED* AL3 2
Tanners Cl *STALW/RED* AL3 2
Tarrant Dr *HARP* AL5 12
Tassell Hall *STALW/RED* AL3 10
Tavistock Av *STAL* AL1 19
Tavistock Cl *STAL* AL1 27
Taylor Cl *STALE/WH* AL4 19
Telford Rd *LCOL/BKTW* AL2 28
Temperance St *STALW/RED* AL3 2
Temple Vw *STALW/RED* AL3 2
Tennyson Rd *HARP* AL5 6
   LCOL/BKTW AL2 26
Tewin Cl *STALE/WH* AL4 19
Thamesdale *LCOL/BKTW* AL2 33
Therfield Rd *STALW/RED* AL3 2
Thirlestane *STAL* AL1 3
Thirlmere Dr *STAL* AL1 28
Thompsons Cl *HARP* AL5 6
Thornbury *HARP* AL5 7
Thornton St *STALW/RED* AL3 2
Thorpefield Cl *STALW/RED* AL3 19
Thorpe Rd *STAL* AL1 23
Thrales End La *HARP* AL5 5

ales End Rd HARP AL5 ....5 H1
worth Wk STALE/WH AL4 ....20 B4
bers Ct HARP AL5 ....6 A4
geys Cl STALW/RED AL3 ....10 D4
ern Cl HARP AL5 ....5 F2
endell La LCOL/BKTW AL2 ....30 D1
e Barn Cl STAL AL1 ....26 D3
rton Ct HARP AL5 * 13 F3
street Wy HARP AL5 ....12 D1
on Ms STALW/RED AL3 ....11 E4
lmin Dr STALW/RED AL3 ....18 D5
ey Cl LCOL/BKTW AL2 ....28 C5
er Hill La STALW/WH AL4 ....15 E5
nsend Av STAL AL1 ....2 E3
nsend Ct HARP AL5 ....6 A5
nsend Dr STALW/RED AL3 ....23 E1
nsend Rd HARP AL5 ....5 H5
elvyn Pl STAL AL1 ....26 D1
mpington Dr STAL AL1 ....27 E2
or Rd STALW/WH AL4 ....14 D1
nells Wy HARP AL5 ....5 G2
rford STALW/WH AL4 ....20 B5
ners Ct HARP AL5 ....5 F5
edale LCOL/BKTW AL2 ....33 E1
enhanger Gn
  TALE/WH AL4 ....28 C2

U

erston Cl STAL AL1 ....3 H6
 Uplands HARP AL5 ....12 B5
er Culver Rd STAL AL1 ....3 G2
er Dagnall St
  TALW/RED AL3 ....2 C5
er Heath Rd STAL AL1 ....3 G2
er Lattimore Rd STAL AL1 ....2 E6
er Marlborough Rd
  TAL AL1 ....2 E6
on Av STALW/RED AL3 ....2 C5
on Cl LCOL/BKTW AL2 ....27 E4

V

e Cl HARP AL5 ....5 G2
e Ct STALE/WH AL4 ....14 C2

Valerie Cl STAL AL1 ....24 A4
Vallance Pl HARP AL5 ....12 D2
Valley Ri STALE/WH AL4 ....7 G4
Valley Rd STALW/RED AL3 ....19 F5
Vanda Crs STAL AL1 ....3 H7
Vaughan Md STALW/RED AL3 ....10 D5
Vaughan Rd HARP AL5 ....6 C5
Ventura Pk LCOL/BKTW AL2 ......31 G3
Ver-Colne Valley Wk STAL AL1 ...27 F1
  ....11 E5
Vernon's Cl STAL AL1 ....2 E7
Ver Rd STALW/RED AL3 ....2 A5
Verulam Rd STALW/RED AL3 ....22 C3
Vesta Av STAL AL1 ....26 D2
Vicarage Cl STAL AL1 ....26 D2
Victoria Rd HARP AL5 ....6 C5
Victoria St STAL AL1 ....2 E6
Victor Smith Ct
  LCOL/BKTW AL2 * 30 B5
Villiers Crs STALE/WH AL4 ....24 C1

W

Waddington Rd STALW/RED AL3 ....2 C5
Waddling La STALE/WH AL4 ....8 D5
Waldegrave Pk HARP AL5 ....7 E5
Walkers Cl HARP AL5 ....12 D2
Walkers Rd HARP AL5 ....12 C2
Wallingford Wk STAL AL1 ....27 E2
Walnut Cl LCOL/BKTW AL2 ....30 C1
Walsingham Wy
  LCOL/BKTW AL2 ....32 B1
Walton St STAL AL1 ....3 G3
Warren Rd STAL AL1 ....26 D3
The Warren HARP AL5 ....12 B4
Warwick Rd STAL AL1 ....3 G2
Waterend La STALE/WH AL4 ....15 H1
  STALW/RED AL3 ....11 E4
Watermeadow STALW/RED AL2 ...31 E2
Waterside LCOL/BKTW AL2 ....32 D1
Watersplash Ct
  LCOL/BKTW AL2 * 33 E1
Watery La STALW/RED AL3 ....4 B3
Watford Rd LCOL/BKTW AL2 .....30 B1
Watling St LCOL/BKTW AL2 ....27 E4
  STAL AL1 ....26 D2
Watling Vw STAL AL1 ....26 D2
Watson Av STALW/RED AL3 ....23 G1
Watson's Wk STAL AL1 ....2 E7
Waveney Rd HARP AL5 ....6 D3

Waverley Rd STALW/RED AL3 ....2 B1
Welbeck Ri HARP AL5 ....13 E3
Welclose St STALW/RED AL3 ....2 B6
Wellington Rd LCOL/BKTW AL2 ...28 C5
  STAL AL1 ....24 A5
Wells Cl HARP AL5 ....5 H2
  STALW/RED AL3 ....2 A3
Wendover Cl HARP AL5 ....7 E5
  STALW/WH AL4 ....20 B4
Wensley Cl HARP AL5 ....13 E3
West Av STALW/RED AL3 ....26 C4
Westbourne Ms STAL AL1 ....2 D6
West Common HARP AL5 ....12 C3
West Common Cl HARP AL5 ....12 C4
West Common Gv HARP AL5 ......12 C4
West Common Wy HARP AL5 .....12 B4
Westfield Av HARP AL5 ....6 B3
Westfield Ct STALE/WH AL4 ....24 C1
Westfield Dr HARP AL5 ....6 C2
Westfield Pl HARP AL5 ....6 C2
Westfield Rd HARP AL5 ....6 C2
Westfields STALW/RED AL3 ....2 A5
Westminster Ct HARP AL5 * 12 D2
  STAL AL1 ....26 D1
Westminster Ldg STAL AL1 * 26 D1
West Riding LCOL/BKTW AL2 .....30 A4
West View Rd STALW/RED AL3 ......2 C4
West Wy HARP AL5 ....6 C2
Weybourne Cl HARP AL5 ....7 E4
Wheat Cl STALE/WH AL4 ....19 H5
Wheatfield Av HARP AL5 ....12 B4
Wheatfield Rd HARP AL5 ....12 A4
Wheathampstead Rd
  HARP AL5 ....13 E1
Wheatleys STALE/WH AL4 ....24 B2
Wheatlock Md STALW/RED AL3 ..10 D4
Whitebeams LCOL/BKTW AL2 ....30 C2
Whitecroft STAL AL1 ....28 A2
White Hedge Dr
  STALW/RED AL3 ....2 A2
White Horse La LCOL/BKTW AL2 ..28 D5
Whitings Cl HARP AL5 ....7 E2
Wick Av STALE/WH AL4 ....14 C1
Wildwood Av LCOL/BKTW AL2 ...30 A4
Wilkin's Green La HAT AL10 ....25 H3
Wilkins Green Ter
  STALE/WH AL4 * 25 G4
Willoughby Rd HARP AL5 ....6 C2
Willowby Cl LCOL/BKTW AL2 .....28 C5
Willow Crs STAL AL1 ....24 B4
Willowside LCOL/BKTW AL2 ......32 D1
The Willows STAL AL1 ....27 H3

Willow Wy HARP AL5 ....6 D2
  STAL AL1 ....30 B1
Wilshere Av STAL AL1 ....6 C3
Wilstone Dr STALE/WH AL4 ....20 B4
Windermere Av STAL AL1 ....24 A5
Windmill Av STALE/WH AL4 ....20 B5
Windridge Cl STALW/RED AL3 ....26 B4
Wingate Wy STAL AL1 ....23 H5
Winton Ter STAL AL1 * 23 F5
Wistaria Dr LCOL/BKTW AL2 ......28 A5
Wistlea Crs STALE/WH AL4 ....29 G1
Withy Pl LCOL/BKTW AL2 ....30 D2
Woodcockhill STALE/WH AL4 .....20 C3
Wood End LCOL/BKTW AL2 ....30 D2
Wood End Hl HARP AL5 ....5 G3
Wood End Rd HARP AL5 ....5 G3
Woodland STALW/RED AL3 * 19 C5
Woodland Dr STALE/WH AL4 ......24 B3
Woodlands HARP AL5 ....5 G3
  LCOL/BKTW AL2 ....30 D1
Woodlea LCOL/BKTW AL2 ....30 A4
Woodside Rd LCOL/BKTW AL2 ...30 A4
Woodstock Rd North STAL AL1 ...24 A4
Woodstock Rd South STAL AL1 ..24 A4
Woodvale Pk STAL AL1 ....24 A4
Woolams STALW/RED AL3 * 10 D5
Woollam Crs STALW/RED AL3 .....18 D5
Woollams STALW/RED AL3 * 10 D5
Wordsworth Rd HARP AL5 ....6 B3
Worley Rd STALW/RED AL3 ....2 C3
Wright Cl STALE/WH AL4 ....14 C2
Wroxham Wy HARP AL5 ....6 D3
Wych Elms LCOL/BKTW AL2 ....30 C2
Wycombe Pl STAL AL1 ....24 A1
Wycombe Wy STALE/WH AL4 .....24 A1
Wyedale LCOL/BKTW AL2 ....33 E1
Wynches Farm Dr
  STALE/WH AL4 ....24 C4
Wynchlands Crs
  STALE/WH AL4 ....24 C4

Y

Yeomans Av HARP AL5 ....5 G3
Yewtree End LCOL/BKTW AL2 ....30 C1
York Rd STAL AL1 ....3 G4
Yule Cl LCOL/BKTW AL2 ....30 A4

Index - featured places

bey Gateway
  TALW/RED AL3 ....2 B6
bey Primary School
  TAL AL1 ....2 B7
bey View Golf Club
  TALW/RED AL3 ....28 C5
oyne Lodge Primary School
  TALW/RED AL3 ....2 C4
an Arena Cinema
  TAL AL1 ....2 D5
wickbury Park Golf Club
  HARP AL5 ....7 F5
wickbury School
  HARP AL5 ....13 F1
ed Business Centre
  HARP AL5 ....6 D3
more House Hotel
  TAL AL1 ....3 G3
quith Court School
  HARP AL5 ....6 A3
chwood Golf Club
  TALW/RED AL3 ....22 C1
chwood School
  STALW/RED AL3 ....23 E1
aumont School
  STALE/WH AL4 ....24 C3
ech Hyde Primary School
  TALE/WH AL4 ....14 C2
nards Heath
nfant School
  TAL AL1 ....3 G1
nards Heath
unior School
  HARP AL5 ....23 F1
cket Wood Sports Centre
  COL/BKTW AL2 ....30 C5
ad Colney Lakes
ature Reserve
  COL/BKTW AL2 ....32 D2
np Primary School
  AL1 ....24 A5

Cathedral & Abbey
Church of St Alban
  STAL AL1 ....2 B6
Christopher Place
Shopping Centre
  STALW/RED AL3 ....2 C5
Clore Shalom School
  RAD WD7 ....32 D4
Colney Heath JMI School
  STALE/WH AL4 ....29 H1
Crabtree J&I School
  HARP AL5 ....6 D5
Crown Prosecution Service
  STAL AL1 ....2 D6
Cunningham Hill J&I School
  STAL AL1 ....27 H1
De Havilland Aircraft
Heritage Centre & Mosquito
Aircraft Museum
  LCOL/BKTW AL2 ....33 G3
Elliswick Lawn Tennis Club
  HARP AL5 ....6 C4
Executive Park
Industrial Estate
  STAL AL1 ....24 A4
Fleetville Junior School
  STAL AL1 ....3 K6
Francis Bacon Maths
& Computing College
  STAL AL1 ....28 A2
Garden Fields JMI School
  STALW/RED AL3 ....23 E1
Gardens of the Rose
(Royal National Rose)
  LCOL/BKTW AL2 ....26 A5
Grebe House Wildlife Centre &
Gardens
  STALW/RED AL3 ....22 C4
Greenwood Park
Leisure Centre
  LCOL/BKTW AL2 ....26 C4

The Grove Infant School
  HARP AL5 ....13 E1
The Grove Junior School
  HARP AL5 ....13 E1
The Gryphon Industrial Park
  STALW/RED AL3 ....19 G5
Haperbury Hospital
  RAD WD7 ....32 B5
Harpenden Common Golf Club
  HARP AL5 ....12 C3
Harpenden Golf Club
  HARP AL5 ....12 A4
Harpenden Health Centre
  HARP AL5 ....6 B4
Harpenden Hospital
  HARP AL5 ....6 B2
Harpenden House Hotel
  HARP AL5 ....12 C1
Harpenden Memorial Hospital
  HARP AL5 ....6 C4
Harpenden RUFC
  HARP AL5 ....11 H3
Harpenden Sports Centre
  HARP AL5 ....12 B1
Harpenden Swimming Pool
  HARP AL5 ....6 B5
Heathlands Special School
  STALW/RED AL3 ....23 F1
Heritage Close
Shopping Centre
  STALW/RED AL3 ....2 B6
Hertfordshire Business Centre
  LCOL/BKTW AL2 ....28 C5
Herts County Agricultural
Showground
  STALW/RED AL3 ....4 B5
High Beeches Primary School
  HARP AL5 ....13 E1
Homewood Independent
School
  LCOL/BKTW AL2 ....30 C2

Horseshoe Business Park
  LCOL/BKTW AL2 ....30 C4
How Wood Primary School
  LCOL/BKTW AL2 ....30 D1
Innkeeper's Lodge
  LCOL/BKTW AL2 ....32 D1
Jubilee Centre
  STALW/RED AL3 ....2 D4
Killigrew Primary School
  LCOL/BKTW AL2 ....26 C4
Kingsbury Watermill Museum
& Waffle House
  STALW/RED AL3 ....22 C2
The Kings School
  HARP AL5 ....6 A2
Lea Industrial Estate
  HARP AL5 ....6 D2
The Lea Primary School
  HARP AL5 ....6 B2
London Colney JMI School
  LCOL/BKTW AL2 ....28 C4
Loreto College
  STAL AL1 ....3 F5
Maltings Arts Theatre
  STAL AL1 ....2 D6
The Maltings Shopping Centre
  STAL AL1 ....2 C6
Mandeville Health Centre
  STAL AL1 ....27 E2
Mandeville Primary School
  STAL AL1 ....27 E2
Manland Primary School
  HARP AL5 ....6 C3
Manor Lodge School
  RAD WD7 ....33 H4
Maple Primary School
  STAL AL1 ....2 E4
Margaret Wix JMI School
  STALW/RED AL3 ....18 D5
Marlborough School
  STAL AL1 ....26 D1

Mid Hertfordshire Golf Club
STALE/WH AL4 ....**8** C2
Nicholas Breakspear RC School
STALE/WH AL4 ....**24** D5
North Orbital Trading Estate
STAL AL1 ....**27** H3
Oaklands College
HARP AL5 ....**6** C5
STAL AL1 ....**3** F5
STALE/WH AL4 ....**24** D3
Oakwood JMI School
STALE/WH AL4 ....**24** B3
Old Verulamiums RFC
LCOL/BKTW AL2 ....**28** B4
Park Industrial Estate
LCOL/BKTW AL2 ....**31** F1
Park Street CE Primary School
LCOL/BKTW AL2 ....**31** E1
Prae Wood Primary School
STALW/RED AL3 ....**22** B5
Premier Travel Inn
LCOL/BKTW AL2 ....**31** E4
Quality Hotel
STAL AL1 ....**27** G1
Ramada Hotel
STALW/RED AL3 ....**16** B1
Redbourn Golf Club
STALW/RED AL3 ....**5** E5
Redbourn Industrial Centre
STALW/RED AL3 ....**11** E4
Redbourn Junior & Infant
School
STALW/RED AL3 ....**10** D4
Redbourn Recreation Centre
STALW/RED AL3 ....**10** D2
Riverside Industrial Estate
HARP AL5 ....**6** D2
LCOL/BKTW AL2 ....**32** D1
Roman Theatre of Verulamium
STALW/RED AL3 ....**22** B4
Roundwood Park School
HARP AL5 ....**5** H4
Roundwood Primary School
HARP AL5 ....**5** H4

Russell Clinic
STALW/RED AL3 ....**2** C5
St Adrians RC Primary School
STAL AL1 ....**26** D2
St Alban & St Stephen RC
Junior/Mixed School
STAL AL1 ....**3** J6
St Albans City FC
STAL AL1 ....**3** G4
St Albans City Hospital
STALW/RED AL3 ....**2** B2
St Albans Girls School
STALW/RED AL3 ....**19** F5
St Albans High School
for Girls
STAL AL1 ....**2** E3
St Albans Lawn Tennis Club
STALE/WH AL4 ....**24** B2
St Albans Museum
STAL AL1 ....**2** E4
St Albans Musical Museum
STALW/RED AL3 ....**30** C2
St Albans Music School
STALW/RED AL3 ....**23** E1
St Albans Organ Museum
STAL AL1 ....**24** A5
St Albans Principal
Health Centre
STAL AL1 ....**2** E5
St Albans Retail Park
STAL AL1 ....**27** E1
St Albans & St Stephens
Infant School
STAL AL1 ....**3** H7
St Albans School
STALW/RED AL3 ....**2** B6
St Bernadette RC
Primary School
LCOL/BKTW AL2 ....**32** C1
St Dominic RC Primary School
HARP AL5 ....**12** C1
St Georges Sch
Technology College
HARP AL5 ....**6** C4

St Helens Primary School
STALE/WH AL4 ....**14** C1
St Hildas School
HARP AL5 ....**6** A4
St John Fisher RC
Primary School
STALE/WH AL4 ....**24** B1
St Lukes Special School
STALW/RED AL3 ....**10** D3
St Michael's Manor Hotel
STALW/RED AL3 ....**22** C4
St Michaels Primary School
STALW/RED AL3 ....**22** B3
St Nicholas Primary School
HARP AL5 ....**6** B5
St Peters JMI School
STAL AL1 ....**23** F5
Salisbury Lawn Tennis Club
STAL AL1 ....**24** A3
Sandridge Gate
Business Centre
STALE/WH AL4 ....**19** G5
STALE/WH AL4 ....**20** A3
Sandridge School
STALE/WH AL4 ....**20** C2
Sandridge Youth Club & Sports
Centre
STALW/RED AL3 ....**20** A3
Sandringham School
STALE/WH AL4 ....**20** A5
Sauncey Wood Primary School
HARP AL5 ....**7** E2
Silk Mill House Museum
STALW/RED AL3 ....**10** D4
Sir John Lawes School
HARP AL5 ....**6** D3
Skyswood JMI School
STALE/WH AL4 ....**24** B1
Smug Oak Green
Business Centre
LCOL/BKTW AL2 ....**30** C3
Sopwell House Hotel,
Country Club & Spa
STAL AL1 ....**27** G3

Southdown Industrial Estate
HARP AL5 ....**12**
Sphere Industrial Estate
STAL AL1 ....**3**
Stags School
STALW/RED AL3 ....**19**
Stroud Wood Business Centre
LCOL/BKTW AL2 ....**31**
Thistle Hotel
LCOL/BKTW AL2 ....**30**
Townsend CE School
STALW/RED AL3 ....**18**
University of Hertfordshire
STAL AL1 ....**2**
University of Hertfordshire
Faculty of Law
STAL AL1 ....**2**
Verulam Golf Club
STAL AL1 ....**27**
Verulam Industrial Estate
STAL AL1 ....**27**
Verulam School
STAL AL1 ....**3**
Verulamium Museum
STALW/RED AL3 ....**22**
Victoria Square Business Area
STAL AL1 ....**3**
Watling View Special School
STAL AL1 ....**27**
Westfield Cemetery
HARP AL5 ....**6**
Westminster Lodge
Leisure Centre & Pool
STAL AL1 ....**26**
Wheatfields J&I School
STALE/WH AL4 ....**20**
Windermere Primary
School
STAL AL1 ....**28**
Wood End School
HARP AL5 ....**5**
Ye Olde Fighting Cocks Inn
STALW/RED AL3 ....**2**

Acknowledgements

Schools address data provided by Education Direct.

Petrol station information supplied by Johnsons

One-way street data provided by © Tele Atlas N.V. Tele Atlas

Garden centre information provided by

Garden Centre Association ⚫ Britains best garden centres

Wyevale Garden Centres 🌷

The statement on the front cover of this atlas is sourced, selected and quoted
from a reader comment and feedback form received in 2004

Discover Britain

with AA travel guides.

London

Britain

AA Travel Guides
Britain's largest travel publisher
order online at www.theAA.com/travel

AA

Notes

AA **Street by Street** QUESTIONNAIRE

Dear Atlas User
Your comments, opinions and recommendations are very important to us.
So please help us to improve our street atlases by taking a few minutes
to complete this simple questionnaire.

You do not need a stamp (unless posted outside the UK). If you do not want to remove
this page from your street atlas, then photocopy it or write your answers on a plain sheet
of paper.

Send to: Marketing Assistant, AA Publishing, 14th Floor Fanum House,
Freepost SCE 4598, Basingstoke RG21 4GY

ABOUT THE ATLAS...

Please state which city / town / county you bought:

_____

Where did you buy the atlas? (City, Town, County)

_____

For what purpose? (please tick all applicable)

To use in your local area ☐   **To use on business or at work** ☐

Visiting a strange place ☐   **In the car** ☐   **On foot** ☐

Other (please state)

_____

Have you ever used any street atlases other than AA Street by Street?

Yes ☐   **No** ☐

If so, which ones?

_____

Is there any aspect of our street atlases that could be improved?
(Please continue on a seperate sheet if necessary)

_____
_____
_____

ML187z

continued overleaf

Please list the features you found most useful:

_____

_____

Please list the features you found least useful:

_____

_____

_____

LOCAL KNOWLEDGE...

Local knowledge is invaluable. Whilst every attempt has been made to make the information contained in this atlas as accurate as possible, should you notice any inaccuracies, please detail them below (if necessary, use a blank piece of paper) or e-mail us at _streetbystreet@theAA.com_

_____

_____

_____

ABOUT YOU...

Name (Mr/Mrs/Ms) _____

Address _____

                                              Postcode _____

Daytime tel no _____

E-mail address _____

Which age group are you in?

Under 25 ☐   **25-34** ☐   **35-44** ☐   **45-54** ☐   **55-64** ☐   **65+** ☐

Are you an AA member?   YES ☐   **NO** ☐

Do you have Internet access?   YES ☐   **NO** ☐

_____

Thank you for taking the time to complete this questionnaire. Please send it to us as soon as possible, and remember, you do not need a stamp (unless posted outside the UK).

We may use information we hold about you to, telephone or email you about other products and services offered by the AA, we do NOT disclose this information to third parties.

Please tick here if you do not wish to hear about products and services from the AA. ☐